I Am Drenched In The Blood of Jesus Christ

I Am Drenched In The Blood of Jesus Christ

Blood Bought, Blood Stained, Blood Washed

Anthony B. Powell

Xulon Elite

Xulon Press Elite
2301 Lucien Way #415
Maitland, FL 32751
407.339.4217
www.xulonpress.com

Unless otherwise indicated, Scripture quotations taken from the King James Version (KJV) –*public domain*.

Paperback ISBN-13: 978-1-66287-196-2
Ebook ISBN-13: 978-1-66287-197-9

CONTENTS

PREFACE

Our Lord Jesus Christ inspired me to write *I Am Drenched in the Blood of Jesus Christ: Blood Bought, Blood Stained, Blood Washed.* The Holy Spirit motivated me to use "drenched in the blood of Jesus Christ" as the foundational concept for this book.

We, as born-again believers, need to truly understand this concept and the significance of being completely soaked and saturated with the precious blood of Jesus Christ. Once we comprehend and personally respond in trust and obedience to the truth of being drenched in the blood of Jesus Christ, we will abundantly walk in the fullness of Him. As this truth consumes you, it fills you with hope, power, strength, authority, and encouragement.

> *Thou waterest the ridges thereof abundantly: thou settlest the furrows thereof: thou makest it soft with showers: thou blessest the springing thereof* (Psalm 65:10).

So, as you read, immerse yourself in *I Am Drenched in the Blood of Jesus Christ: Blood Bought, Blood Stained, Blood Washed* and watch the newness take shape in your heart. Allow the truth of God's Word to take root in your soul.

> *My doctrine shall drop as the rain, my speech shall distil as the dew, as the small rain upon the tender herb, and as the showers upon the grass: Because I will publish the name of the Lord: ascribe ye greatness unto our God* (Deut. 32:2-3).

ACKNOWLEDGMENTS

I wish to acknowledge my wife, Angela, for her patience and understanding during the writing and publishing of this book, *I Am Drenched in the Blood of Jesus Christ: Blood Bought, Blood Stained, Blood Washed.*

> *For though you have ten thousand instructors in Christ, yet have you not many fathers: for in Christ Jesus I have begotten you through the gospel* (1 Corinthians 4:15).

Spiritually minded and having a well-rounded spiritual life are essential to our spiritual growth and maturity. Though we have many who offer their services as our instructors, we have only one who is our spiritual father. That one person in my life is Bishop Rodney S. Walker, Heritage Church International, and General Overseer, Bishop R S Walker Ministries. I acknowledge Bishop Walker for his dedication and commitment to my spiritual growth, pouring out into me, developing an intimate father-son relationship, and bringing and releasing me into the Office of the Prophet.

I also acknowledge two other wonderful people who have had a spiritual significance in my spiritual life, growth, and maturity. First, my pastor, Bishop Melvin E. Blake, JR, In His Imagine Christian Ministries. Bishop Blake's leadership, love for the people of God, compassion, and nurturing nature are truly a Godsend and blessings to the Body of Christ. I acknowledge and thank Bishop Blake for the last twenty-three years for his pastoral care, providing a spiritual covering, occasions to preach and teach the gospel, and opportunities to function in a leadership role. Second, Reverend Doctor Joseph E. Powell, JR, Covenant Lifehouse Ministries. My brother in Jesus Christ, as well as my natural brother and fondly known as 'Poochie' for his ability to uniquely blend humor and wit with the Word of God to impact and change lives for the glory and kingdom of God.

INTRODUCTION

Our fundamental understanding of *I Am Drenched in the Blood of Jesus Christ, Blood Bought, Blood Stained, Blood Washed* begins with our realization that there is a tremendous difference between being drenched and sprinkled in the blood of Jesus Christ. God wants to completely soak/saturate us with the blood of Jesus Christ until the Spirit, without measure, oozes through us with the power, authority, and strength of the Godhead who dwells bodily in us.

We must fully understand that when Jesus Christ drenches us in His blood, it baptizes us into the power, authority, might, and strength of His Holy Spirit. This drenching allows us to engage in spiritual warfare boldly, fully, and effectively.

Jesus Christ drenches you in His blood to make your name known before your adversaries so they may tremble at your very presence! That is why Satan, demons, and the whole host of demonic forces will do everything possible to keep you distracted by sending people or ideas to confuse you or plant seeds of doubt to hide the truth to ensure you are not aware and ignorant of the fact that you are drenched in the blood of Jesus Christ.

We can only fully understand what it is to be drenched in the blood of Jesus Christ by comprehending that we are *Blood Bought, Blood Stained, and Blood Washed.*

Our fundamental understanding of *I Am Drenched in the Blood of Jesus Christ: Blood Bought, Blood Stained, Blood Washed* concludes with pleading the blood of Jesus Christ.

What is pleading the blood? Pleading the blood activates what happened through the shed blood of Jesus Christ at the cross when He *drenched, blood-bought, blood-stained, and blood-washed* us in His precious blood. When we plead the blood, we ask God to provide what Jesus Christ's blood has already purchased, the great exchange provided by Jesus Christ, and it is at the cross that Jesus Christ offered us the most amazing deal in eternity. In essence, pleading the blood is a statement of faith about what happened at Calvary.

Chapter 1
THE BLOOD OF ABEL
AND THE BLOOD OF
JESUS CHRIST

I Am Drenched in the Blood of Jesus Christ begins with an appreciation for the blood of Abel and the blood of Jesus Christ. To understand the blood of Abel and the blood of Jesus Christ, we need to first consider God's view of blood. God, our Father, places great importance on blood and forbids eating blood, for the life of the flesh is in the blood (Lev 17:11).

Blood sprinkled on the altar makes an atonement for the soul (Lev. 17:11). This is clearly evident when Jesus Christ instituted the Lord's Supper. He stated, *"For this is my blood of the new testament, which is shed for many for the remission of sins"* (Matt. 26:28).

God originated a covenant when He made coats of skin and clothed Adam and Eve. God made this covenant with blood, for without shedding blood, the remission of sins cannot happen. In the same way, our Father paid a price through Jesus Christ's shed blood to manifest His grace and adopt us as His sons.

The significance of Jesus Christ's blood is the central force of truth running throughout the entire Word of God. When accepted, Jesus Christ's blood atones for and redeems us from our sins.

Abel's Blood

Cain first shed blood when he drew his brother, Abel, into the field and killed him. At that moment, perhaps Cain thought his worries were over because the ground swallowed up Abel's blood. But the Scriptures proved Cain wrong, for the voice of Abel's blood cried from the ground and echoed loudly in God's attentive ears.

> *And he said, What hast thou done? the voice of thy brother's blood crieth unto me from the ground* (Gen. 4:10).

The blood of Abel cried out because of the following principle, which runs throughout Scripture, "*The life of the flesh is in the blood*" (Lev. 17:11). Abel was innocent of wrongdoing, and that created a loud voice to the silent, red pool saturating the soil around his fatally injured body.

Abel's blood crying from the ground did not seek a mediator but went directly to God's judgment seat and accused the very one who murdered him—his brother, Cain. We can only imagine what Abel's blood cried out to the Almighty God, but rest assured the voice of Abel's blood spoke. God heard it, and when He heard it, he immediately reckoned with Cain and said, *"What have you done"*(Gen.4:10)?

The Blood of Abel and the Blood of Jesus Christ Spoke

What we need to notice about the blood of Abel and the blood of Jesus Christ is that they both spoke. We witness in Hebrews 11:4, though dead, Abel's blood still speaks because of his faith in blood atonement and to men today of such a need.

It is such a great comfort to know the blood of Jesus Christ speaks and pleads before the eternal throne. All blood has a voice, for God is jealous of its preservation, but the voice of the blood of Jesus Christ far surpasses all.

> *By faith Abel offered unto God a more excellent sacrifice than Cain, by which he obtained witness that he was righteous, God testifying of his gifts: and by it he being dead yet speaketh* (Heb. 11:4).

> *And to Jesus the mediator of the new covenant, and to the blood of sprinkling, that speaketh better things than that of Abel* (Heb. 12:24).

3

Furthermore, we must always remember, even though Abel's blood spoke as it fell to the ground, his blood simply foreshadowed the more glorious substance to which Jesus Christ's death and shed blood assure us. We must comprehend that Jesus Christ died not to typify atonement but offered it. Jesus Christ did not represent sacrifice. He was the great sacrifice itself and inasmuch as the substance must always exceed the foreshadowing, the blood of Jesus Christ speaks louder and better things than the blood of Abel.

The Blood of Jesus Christ Speaks Better Things!

The blood of Jesus Christ speaks better things than the blood of Abel because our Lord Jesus Christ's blood cries out for our forgiveness, clemency, redemption, and salvation.

Jesus Christ's blood does not ask for vindication. Instead, His blood demands forgiveness, an intimate relationship with God, and a future for us, adopted into God's own family and made heirs of God and co-heirs with Jesus Christ.

His blood now speaks for us and washes us from all sin! This means God not only forgives our past sins but for anything we do now, we can appropriate the blood of Jesus Christ.

When we repent, we come into agreement with what the blood speaks. Realize that repentance is essential to agreeing with the blood of Jesus Christ! Repentance brings things to the light, allowing us to come out of darkness, choose light over darkness, see the difference between Satan and God, and choose God over Satan.

It is the blood that washes us from all sin from the time of confession of sin and as long as we walk in the light. It is the blood that makes us a new creature in Jesus Christ and sets us free from our past, causing old things to pass away and all things become new.

> *To open their eyes, and to turn them from darkness to light, and from the power of Satan unto God, that they may receive forgiveness of sins, and inheritance among them which are sanctified by faith that is in me* (Acts 26:18).

> *Who hath delivered us from the power of darkness, and hath translated us into the kingdom of his dear Son: In whom we have redemption through his blood, even the forgiveness of sins* (Col. 1:13–14).

> *If we say that we have fellowship with him, and walk in darkness, we lie, and do not the truth: But if we walk in the light, as he is in the light, we have fellowship one with another, and the blood of Jesus Christ his Son cleanseth us from all sin. If we say that we have no sin, we deceive ourselves, and the truth is not in us. If we confess our sins, he is faithful and just to forgive us our sins, and to cleanse us from all unrighteousness. If we say that we have not sinned, we*

make him a liar, and his word is not in us (1 John 1:6–10).

It is paramount to understand it is Jesus Christ's blood that grants God the legal right to forgive us. The heart of God is to forgive. He just needed the legal right to do it. Jesus Christ's blood granted God that legal right. Furthermore, Jesus Christ's blood continually speaks today and perpetually calls down justice and mercy from the throne of our Almighty Father and the courts of heaven.

CHAPTER 2
THE BLOOD OF JESUS CHRIST IS SIGNIFICANT

T he blood of Jesus Christ is significant and is another aspect involved in our fundamental understanding for *I Am Drenched in the Blood of Jesus Christ: Blood Bought, Blood Stained, Blood Washed.*

As we grasp the implication of blood as expressed in Scripture, we come to know the significance of the blood of Jesus Christ. Blood is mentioned throughout the Bible, starting with the first blood covering (Gen. 3:21), continuing through the law of Moses with the offering of the blood of sacrifices, and ending with the sacrifice of the Lamb of God, Jesus Christ, who purchased the church[1] with His own blood!

---

[1] Strong's #1577: ἐκκλησία ekklēsía (pronounced ek-klay-see>-ah); from a compound of G1537 and a derivative of G2564; a calling out, i.e. (concretely) a popular meeting, especially a religious congregation (Jewish synagogue, or Christian community of members on earth or saints in heaven or both): —assembly, church

Take heed therefore unto yourselves, and to all the flock, over the which the Holy Ghost hath made you overseers, to feed the church of God, which he hath purchased with his own blood (Acts 20:28).

God Places Great Emphasis on Blood.

A close examination of blood reveals that God places great emphasis on it. Why? In the Old Testament blood, foreshadowing the sacrifice of Jesus Christ was the key component in the atonement system God instituted. Blood represents life, which is sacred to God.

We must understand God is so obsessed with blood because He's so obsessed with life. The Bible regards blood as the symbol and source of life.

For the life of the flesh is in the blood: and I have given it to you upon the altar to make an atonement for your souls: for it is the blood that maketh an atonement for the soul (Lev. 17:11).

For it is the life of all flesh; the blood of it is for the life thereof: therefore I said unto the children of Israel, Ye shall eat the blood of no manner of flesh: for the life of all flesh is the blood thereof: whosoever eateth it shall be cut off (Lev. 17:14).

In Genesis 3:21, God made a divine provision to cover Adam and Eve by making coats of skin and clothing them. This first shedding of blood points to our promised Redeemer, Jesus Christ! Then in Exodus 24:6–8, God made a blood covenant (Mosaic covenant) with Moses when he sprinkled half of the blood on the altar and the other half on the people of Israel. It is easy to see that the blood of animals was used in all offerings for sin as man's vicarious substitute (atonement) under the Mosaic (Old Testament) law[2].

Due to its relationship to life, blood signifies the supreme offering to God. God's holiness and justice demand the punishment of sin. The only penalty or payment for sin is eternal death. The offering of an animal and even our own death are not sufficient sacrifices to pay for sin. Atonement requires a perfect, spotless sacrifice offered in just the right way.

A Covenant Was Not Made without Blood

A covenant was not made without blood, as there is not a remission of sins without the shedding of blood. The old covenant of the Old Testament restricted personal approach to God, and services rendered by the priests could not even cleanse the priests who daily and annually offered up sacrifice,

---

[2] Mosaic law – the ancient law of the Hebrews, ascribed to Moses; the part of the Scripture containing this law; the Pentateuch (the first five books of the Old Testament: Genesis, Exodus, Leviticus, Numbers, and Deuteronomy). Source: https://www.dictionary.com/browse/mosaic-law (Accessed May 2, 2021).

first for his own sins and then for the people (Heb. 7:27). Furthermore, the old covenant sacrifices were carnal, temporary, and powerless to cleanse from sin and were only a shadow of the realities of the new covenant.

> *For the law having a shadow of good things to come, and not the very image of the things, can never with those sacrifices which they offered year by year continually make the comers thereunto perfect. For then would they not have ceased to be offered? because that the worshippers once purged should have had no more conscience of sins. But in those sacrifices there is a remembrance again made of sins every year. For it is not possible that the blood of bulls and of goats should take away sins* (Heb. 10:1–4).

However, the sacrifice of the Lamb of God, Jesus Christ, brought new life into being for humanity by atoning us in a manner completely beyond human abilities. Jesus Christ's precious blood atoned for our sins, and His shed blood alone redeems us.

> *For this is my blood of the new testament, which is shed for many for the remission of sins* (Matt. 26:28).

Jesus Christ, the everlasting sacrifice, paid the ransom for our sins. He became our eternal High Priest, entering heaven (the Holy of Holies), once and for all, not by the blood of sacrificial animals but by His own precious blood shed on the cross. Jesus Christ poured out His life in the ultimate atoning sacrifice for our sins and the sins of the world. Jesus Christ paid a ransom!

> *Forasmuch as ye know that ye were not redeemed with corruptible things, as silver and gold, from your vain conversation received by tradition from your fathers; But with the precious blood of Christ, as of a lamb without blemish and without spot* (1 Pet. 1:18–19).

The blood of Jesus Christ established our eternal salvation and created the new covenant. In the New Testament, the blood of Jesus Christ, therefore, becomes the foundation for God's new covenant of grace. Also, at the Last Supper, we observe Jesus Christ convey to His disciples that the cup is the new covenant written in His blood poured out for us.

> *And to Jesus the mediator of the new covenant, and to the blood of sprinkling, that speaketh better things than that of Abel* (Heb. 12:24).

> *Likewise also the cup after supper, saying, This cup is the new testament in my blood, which is shed for you* (Luke 22:20).

Let us remember the old covenant had many sacrifices and was dedicated by the blood of animals, whereas the new covenant has only one sacrifice and is dedicated by the blood of Jesus Christ Himself.

> *By the which will we are sanctified through the offering of the body of Jesus Christ once for all* (Heb. 10:10).

> *For by one offering he hath perfected for ever them that are sanctified* (Heb. 10:14).

The new covenant of Jesus Christ is superior to the old covenant. The old covenant was faulty and done away with for the arrival of the new covenant. The new covenant, unlike the old covenant, provides salvation and eternal life.

> *For if that first covenant had been faultless, then should no place have been sought for the second. For finding fault with them, he saith, Behold, the days come, saith the Lord, when I will make a new covenant with the house of Israel and with the house of Judah: Not according to the covenant that I made with*

their fathers in the day when I took them by the hand to lead them out of the land of Egypt; because they continued not in my covenant, and I regarded them not, saith the Lord. For this is the covenant that I will make with the house of Israel after those days, saith the Lord; I will put my laws into their mind, and write them in their hearts: and I will be to them a God, and they shall be to me a people: And they shall not teach every man his neighbour, and every man his brother, saying, Know the Lord: for all shall know me, from the least to the greatest. For I will be merciful to their unrighteousness, and their sins and their iniquities will I remember no more. In that he saith, A new covenant, he hath made the first old. Now that which decayeth and waxeth old is ready to vanish away (Heb. 8:7–13).

Additionally, the new covenant is superior to the old covenant because of the access it provides to God Almighty. Jesus Christ, as our High Priest, does not minister in an earthly tabernacle or offer the blood of goats and calves, which cannot take away sins. Jesus Christ ministers in the holy place in heaven where He offered the true atonement, His own blood, once and for all, which brings eternal redemption and does not have to make a daily atonement as earthy priests did in the old covenant.[3]

We see the superiority of the new covenant in its accomplishment. Under the old covenant, the blood of goats and bulls and the ashes of a young cow could cleanse people's bodies from ceremonial impurity. Just think how much more, under the new covenant, Jesus Christ's blood purifies our consciences from sinful deeds.

> *But Christ being come an high priest of good things to come, by a greater and more perfect tabernacle, not made with hands, that is to say, not of this building; Neither by the blood of goats and calves, but by his own blood he entered in once into the holy place, having obtained eternal redemption for us. For if the blood of bulls and of goats, and the ashes of an heifer sprinkling the unclean, sanctifieth to the purifying of the flesh: How much more shall the blood of Christ, who through the eternal Spirit offered himself without spot to God, purge your conscience from dead works to serve the living God?* (Heb. 9:11–14).

---

[3]   Dake, Finis, Jennings. *Dake's Annotated Reference Bible* (Ninth Printing edition). (Lawrenceville: Dake Publishing, Inc, 2006), 439, notes j and k.

Another reason the new covenant is superior to the old covenant is Jesus Christ became the mediator of the new covenant, and it is through His death we are given an eternal inheritance and sins are remitted. Consequently, there is not any longer a need for an offering for sins. Jesus Christ's offering is effective for all past, present, and future sins but on condition of proper confession of sin and meeting the terms of continued grace.[4]

> *And for this cause he is the mediator of the new testament, that by means of death, for the redemption of the transgressions that were under the first testament, they which are called might receive the promise of eternal inheritance* (Heb. 9:15).

> *Now where remission of these is, there is no more offering for sin* (Heb. 10:18).

Yet another reason for the new covenant's superiority is we are sanctified through His precious blood shed for us.

> *By the which will we are sanctified through the offering of the body of Jesus Christ once for all* (Heb. 10:10).

---

[4] Romans 10:9-10 and 1 John 1:9

It should be evident that Jesus Christ's death was necessary to make (ratify) the new covenant with man. Since we were under the penalty of death for our sins, and the covenant had to do with the redemption of our sins by the death of a substitute, it was necessary for the one making the covenant to die. The covenant could only be in force after Jesus Christ's death and the covenant ratified by His death.

> *For where a testament is, there must also of necessity be the death of the testator. For a testament is of force after men are dead: otherwise it is of no strength at all while the testator liveth* (Heb. 9:16–17).

The Significance of the Blood of Jesus Christ

The significance of the blood of Jesus Christ is also evident in John 6:54 and 1 Corinthians 11:23–26. In these verses, the Word of God tells believers to partake of Jesus Christ's body and blood. Eating and drinking are figuratively used to partaking in the benefits[5] of Jesus Christ's death. We partake by faith and enjoy the benefits because God gives them to us based on what Jesus Christ did for us. Eating is used figuratively to partaking of spiritual food. In fact, Jesus Christ referred to Himself as *the bread of life.*[6] Jesus Christ is the

---

[5] *Chapter 7* examines these benefits in detail.

[6] John 6:35

heavenly bread, the true life-sustaining power. Anything else is an inadequate substitute. As the bread from heaven, Jesus Christ is our ultimate source of nourishment in life. If we do not eat of this bread, then we will spiritually starve.

> *Whoso eateth my flesh, and drinketh my blood, hath eternal life; and I will raise him up at the last day* (John 6:54).

> *For I have received of the Lord that which also I delivered unto you, that the Lord Jesus the same night in which he was betrayed took bread: And when he had given thanks, he brake it, and said, Take, eat: this is my body, which is broken for you: this do in remembrance of me. After the same manner also he took the cup, when he had supped, saying, this cup is the new testament in my blood: this do ye, as oft as ye drink it, in remembrance of me. For as often as ye eat this bread, and drink this cup, ye do shew the Lord's death till he come* (1 Cor. 11:23–26).

Let us examine the significance of the blood of Jesus Christ and our new position in Jesus Christ because of His precious blood. Our position and the tenfold present state as Christians are obvious in Ephesians 2:13–22:

1. We are in Christ (v. 13)
2. Made near to God (v. 13)
3. Have peace with God (v. 14)
4. Made both one in Christ; Jews and Gentiles make the New Testament Church (vv. 14–16; 3:6; 1 Cor. 12:13)[7]
5. Made part of the church (v. 15–16);
6. Reconciled both Jews and Gentiles to God in one body (v. 16)
7. Access[8] to God by one Spirit (v. 18; 3:12)
8. Fellow citizens with the saints and of the household of God (v. 19)
9. Built upon the foundation of the apostles and prophets and the true foundation, Jesus Christ, the chief cornerstone (v. 20; 1 Cor. 3:11)
10. A habitation of God through the Spirit (v. 22)

---

[7] Matthew 16:18 first mentions the New Testament Church: "*upon this rock I will build my church . . .,*" one church, the body of Jesus Christ, consisting of all born-again believers.

[8] Strong's #4318: προσαγωγή, ῆς, ἡ prosagoge (pronounced pros-ag-ogue-ay'); from 4317 (compare 72); admission: —access

CHAPTER 3
THE ROAD TO CALVARY

Our fundamental understanding continues with our gratitude for what Jesus Christ won for us on the road to Calvary.

Gratitude is our thankfulness to the Lord. We should continually give thanks to Him, regardless of what happens in our lives.

> *In every thing give thanks: for this is the will of God in Christ Jesus concerning you* (1 Thessalonians 5:18).

We can have thankful hearts toward God even when we do not feel thankful for the circumstance or problem. Realize we can grieve – yet remain thankful! We can hurt – yet remain thankful! We can be angry at sin – yet remain thankful! The Bible calls this a "sacrifice of praise" (Hebrews 13:15). Understand, thanking God keeps our hearts in the right relationship with Him and protects us from harmful emotions and attitudes that rob us of the peace God wants us to experience (Philippians 4:6–7).

We should thank God for His Word, believe the Word, and actively stand on the Word, His protection and His joy. Paul and Silas illustrated this during their imprisonment.

> *And at midnight Paul and Silas prayed, and sang praises unto God: and the prisoners heard them* (Acts 16:25).

Paul and Silas remembered the Lord and what the Lord said in His Word. Therefore, what Paul and Silas were praying and singing about was that the Almighty would keep them in every place they went and never leave nor forsake them. Paul and Silas, despite their harsh conditions and the darkness of the dungeon, boldly prayed and sang that God is with us. Paul and Silas, in their mind and heart, knew the Lord Almighty was there in prison with and sitting next to them. Paul and Silas were confident that the Lord would keep them in every place that they went and all they had to do was look around the inner prison and there the Lord Almighty would be. Even in the darkness of the dungeon the Lord is with and keeps them. Paul and Silas knew in their hearts even though their feet were in the stocks, the Lord was right there next to them. Paul and Silas were not concerned with their situation or the harsh treatment they received and even in the darkness of the dungeon they saw the living Lord God Almighty's light.

The word *Calvary* appears in Luke 23:33. It means "skull" (https://www.gotquestions.org/place-of-the-skull.html) and refers to the skull-like hill on which Jesus Christ was crucified. Calvary is also known as Golgotha.[9]

The road to Calvary was a prelude to our being drenched in the blood of Jesus Christ, where we witness a conversation between God the Father and Jesus Christ the Son.

> *These words spake Jesus, and lifted up his eyes to heaven, and said, Father, the hour is come; glorify thy Son, that thy Son also may glorify thee* (John 17:1).

> *I have glorified thee on the earth: I have finished the work which thou gavest me to do* (John 17:4).

The exact moment Jesus Christ uttered these words point us to the cross, His impending death on the cross, and the cross where Jesus Christ blood-bought, blood-stained, blood-washed us. A study of John 17 provides us with further knowledge of what Jesus Christ did and won for us on the road to Calvary. It is not enough to know what Jesus Christ won before Calvary—we need to stand on it!

---

9   Golgotha is the Aramaic name of the location where Jesus Christ was crucified outside of Old Jerusalem. https://www.gotquestions.org/Golgotha-Calvary.html

Let us begin our study of John 17 by first focusing on the word *that*. The Greek word *hina*[10] translates into the English word *that*. Oftentimes *that* signals the content of what is being said. However, a clause beginning with *that* usually speaks of purpose. *That* occurred twenty-three times in Jesus Christ's prayer. His prayer was full of purpose. For example, in John 17:1 Jesus Christ said, *"Father, the hour is come; glorify thy Son, that thy Son also may glorify thee."* In this verse, we see Jesus Christ's request is to glorify thy Son and His purpose is that He may glorify the Father.

On the road to Calvary, Jesus Christ prayed His longest recorded prayer. The purpose of His prayer was unselfish, and His dominant motive was to glorify God in His coming death and resurrection.

We can categorize Jesus Christ's prayer into three parts, and a close examination of each part reveals what Jesus Christ won for us while on the road to Calvary:

- Jesus Christ prays for Himself (17:1–5),

- Jesus Christ prays for His disciples (17:6–19; 25–26), and

---

[10] Strong's #2443: hina (pronounced hin'-ah); probably from the same as the former part of 1438 (through the demonstrative idea; compare 3588); in order that (denoting the purpose or the result): —albeit, because, to the intent (that), lest, so as, (so) that, (for) to. Compare 3363

- Jesus Christ prays for other believers, the church (17:20–26).

Jesus Christ Prays for Himself (17:1–5)

Eternal Life (vv. 2–3, 5)

Jesus prayed for the restoration of His former life He had before *the world was* and eternal life for the believers God gave Him. As Jesus Christ died for all, He can give eternal life to all if all meet the conditions. To know God eternally is eternal life (to spend eternity with the Lord) and is strongly connected with the Lord Jesus Christ

A person's ignorance of Jesus Christ and refusal to know and believe in Him will ultimately condemn the individual. This is what will damn the soul. It is a free choice, whether one accepts eternal life or not.

Jesus Christ Prays for His Disciples (17:6–19; 25–26)

Words (vv. 8, 14)

Jesus Christ prayed, "*For I have given unto them the words which thou gavest me. I have given them thy word.*" (John 17:8). The word *schema* involves Jesus Christ saying the Word, God approving the Word and the Holy Spirit manifesting the Word.

Realize victory cannot happen without words. Our part is to realize we have the Word, seek the Word, receive the

Word, believe the Word, and actively stand on the Word. What good is having the Word if we do not speak it? In fact, Deuteronomy 30:14 states, *"But the word is very nigh unto thee, in thy mouth, and in thy heart, that thou mayest do it."*[11]

Oneness/Unity (vv. 10–11)

Jesus Christ prayed for a sense of oneness and unity. In other words, Jesus Christ wanted His disciples united in purpose.

Protection (v. 11)

Jesus Christ prayed for His disciples' protection from Satan, who is bitterly opposed to the things of God. We can interpret verse 11 as Jesus Christ saying, "While I was with them, I protected them. Now I need you, Father, to protect them."

Joy (v. 13)

Jesus Christ prayed *"that they might have my joy fulfilled in themselves."* Jesus Christ, essentially reminded the disciples *"for the joy of the LORD is your strength" (Nehemiah 8:10)*. We, as believers, need to receive, believe and stand on this fact.

---

[11] Compare Romans 10:8.

24

Oftentimes people confuse joy with happiness. It behooves us to know the difference between these two. First, happiness is an emotion in which we experience feelings ranging from contentment and satisfaction to bliss and intense pleasure. In contrast, joy is a fruit of the Spirit and is what the Holy Spirit produces in the life of a believer.[12] Joy is complete in the Lord Jesus Christ and is an inward stability to stay or stand. Consequently, since the Holy Spirit is the true source of joy, it has nothing to do with what happens or does not happen to you.

Therefore, as true believers, we must not let our circumstances, trials, problems, or troubles hold us captive and realize without a shadow of a doubt that we bear in our body the dying of the Lord Jesus that the life of Jesus might also be made manifest in our body.

It's in our best interest to rejoice in the Lord and make it a lifestyle. Apostle Paul had the right idea, and we should follow the lesson he placed before us when he emphatically stated:

> *As sorrowful, yet alway rejoicing; as poor, yet making many rich; as having nothing, and yet possessing all things* (2 Cor. 6:10).

> *Rejoice in the Lord always: and again I say, Rejoice* (Phil. 4:4).

---

[12] Galatians 5:22

Apostle Paul knew that even when our hearts ache, we still have joy. Paul encouraged us to let our rejoicing be independent of our circumstances because the joy of the Lord is our strength to face all of life's challenges and difficulties. Negative circumstances are temporary, and we do not need to prolong them or make them permanent by our wrong attitude and thinking!

> *We are troubled on every side, yet not distressed; we are perplexed, but not in despair; Persecuted, but not forsaken; cast down, but not destroyed; Always bearing about in the body the dying of the Lord Jesus, that the life also of Jesus might be made manifest in our body. For we which live are always delivered unto death for Jesus' sake, that the life also of Jesus might be made manifest in our mortal flesh* (2 Cor. 4:8–11).

Never give up and always remember and meditate on these Scriptures:

> *God is our refuge and strength, a very present help in trouble* (Ps. 46:1).

> *From the end of the earth will I cry unto thee, when my heart is overwhelmed: lead me to the rock that is higher than I* (Ps. 61:2).

*He only is my rock and my salvation; he is my
defence; I shall not be greatly moved. For thou
hast been a shelter for me, and a strong tower
from the enemy* (Ps. 62:2–3).

*I will say of the Lord, He is my refuge and my
fortress: my God; in him will I trust* (Ps. 91:2).

*I will lift up mine eyes unto the hills, from
whence cometh my help. My help cometh from
the Lord, which made heaven and earth. He
will not suffer thy foot to be moved: he that
keepeth thee will not slumber* (Ps. 121:1–3).

Kept From All Evil (v. 15)

Jesus Christ prayed not to take us out of the world or even
out of our storm/test/trials but that God the Father keep us as
we go through from the evil/wicked one. Jesus Christ wants
us to live as lights and examples of God in the world to glorify
Him.[13] It is important to note that if we want to know how to
convince the world of Jesus Christ, we need to become one as
God and Jesus Christ. The secret is oneness/unity!

---

[13] Matthew 5:16

Sanctify Them (vv. 17–19)

Jesus Christ prayed for a setting apart of believers to a world ministry by the truth.[14]

Jesus Christ Prays for Other Believers, the Church (17:20–26).

Oneness/Unity (vv. 20–21)

In His final petition, Jesus Christ prayed for unity, as God and Jesus Christ were one of all believers in subsequent generations. In fact, Jesus Christ prayed for absolute unity five times (vv. 11, 21–23). The oneness He requested was a spiritual unity, which is visibly manifested in the life of the church and bears witness to His divine mission. The church's unity will reach its consummation in heaven (vv. 24–26), and it is every believer's responsibility to choose to participate in this unity by loving other members of the body of Christ.[15]

Glory (vv. 22, 24)

Jesus Christ prayed for the glorification of all believers and that we may behold His glory, which God gave Him. In

---

[14] John 10:36

[15] *Oneness Note,* Hayford, Jack, *Spirit Filled Life Bible for Students*, New King James Version, (Nashville: Thomas Nelson Publishers, 1982), 1381.

turn, He gave us glory[16] and we need to expose the glory that rests upon us and fill the earth with God's glory.

> *For, behold, the darkness shall cover the earth, and gross darkness the people: but the Lord shall arise upon thee, and his glory shall be seen upon thee* (Isa. 60:2).

> *For the earth shall be filled with the knowledge of the glory of the Lord, as the waters cover the sea* (Hab. 2:14).

A word of caution, we are not to take God's glory as our own. God rests His glory upon us to establish us as a heavyweight in spiritual matters. God will not give the praise and honor due Him to angels, demons, men, or idols. We must not take any glory for ideas, doctrines, works, wisdom, power, or ability that have come from God for His glory.

> *I am the Lord: that is my name: and my glory will I not give to another, neither my praise to graven images* (Isa. 42:8).

---

[16] Strong's #H3519: כָּבוֹד kâbôwd, kaw-bode'; rarely כָּבֹד kâbôd; from H3513; properly, weight, but only figuratively in a good sense, splendor or copiousness:—glorious(-ly), glory, honour(-able). Blue Letter Bible. (https://www.blueletterbible.org/lang/lexicon/lexicon.cfm?t=kjv&strongs=h3519)

In summary, on the road to Calvary, what Jesus Christ did and won for us involved:

- Eternal Life

- Words

- Oneness/Unity

- Protection

- Joy

- Kept from All Evil

- Sanctify Them

- Glory

CHAPTER 4
A PLACE CALLED CALVARY

O ur fundamental understanding continues with our gratitude for the significance of a place called Calvary. We must explicitly apprehend that Calvary was not an afterthought for God nor a death penalty conceived by mankind. Calvary was God's plan conceived in eternity past and a foreordained place where His Son would die as the Savior of mankind. It pleased Jehovah God to permit Jesus Christ's crucifixion at Calvary to bring about redemption and salvation.

Furthermore, it gave God pleasure to see all creation redeemed and restored in right standing and relationship to Himself as before the rebellions of Lucifer and Adam. We must fully realize the eternal purpose, which God purposed in Christ Jesus our Lord, is to have creations of free moral agents who have been thoroughly tested and purged of all possibility of rebellion so that God can show the exceeding riches of His grace toward them in all the ages to come without fear of eternal rebellions.

Also, understand it was the travail of His soul for our restoration and dominion as before the fall.[17] This is what Isaiah 53:10–11 means when it states:

> *Yet it pleased the Lord to bruise him; he hath put him to grief: when thou shalt make his soul an offering for sin, he shall see his seed, he shall prolong his days, and the pleasure of the Lord shall prosper in his hand. He shall see of the travail of his soul, and shall be satisfied: by his knowledge shall my righteous servant justify many; for he shall bear their iniquities. Therefore will I divide him a portion with the great, and he shall divide the spoil with the strong; because he hath poured out his soul unto death: and he was numbered with the transgressors; and he bare the sin of many, and made intercession for the transgressors* (Isa. 53:10–12).

God predestined a place called Calvary, the place of Christ Jesus's crucifixion as a place where:

- **Amazing grace was shown for the entire world to see.** Ephesians 2:8–9 tells us, *"For by grace are ye saved through*

---

[17] Dake, Finis, Jennings, *Dake's Annotated Reference Bible* (Ninth Printing edition), (Lawrenceville: Dake Publishing, Inc, 2006), 1204, notes n, o and p.

Faith; and that not of yourselves: it is the gift of God: Not of works, lest any man should boast." Furthermore, in 2 Corinthians 5:14, we witness that Jesus Christ did not die for a select few but for all mankind. Therefore, we can rightly conclude that grace is not based on family, nationality, race, who you know or do not know, or what you have or do not have. Jesus Christ extends His grace to all!

- **Sin's price was paid in full.** Romans 6:23 tells us, *"For the wages of sin is death; but the gift of God is eternal life through Jesus Christ our Lord."* Then we find in 1 Corinthians 6:20; 7:23 that we are blood-bought with a price. Jesus Christ's precious shed blood is the legal currency with which Jesus Christ purchased our victory. Hebrews 10:19–23 also reminds us Jesus Christ's blood was the currency Jesus Christ poured out (in obedience to the Father) that bought us access to God Himself. We need to recognize the transaction for our souls was made at Calvary, and our debt was paid in full there.

- **Destinies are determined.** Luke 23:27 tells us, *"And there followed him a great company of people, and of women, which also bewailed and lamented him."* The hypocrites, unreasonable, pessimist and passionate, compassionate and cowardly, self-righteous and unrighteous, frivolous and ambitious, curious and questioners, and repentant and unrepentant were there. On that day, all of mankind was represented. Additionally, it is noteworthy to understand that the two men who hung on crosses on either side of Jesus Christ represented all of mankind: one who rejected Christ Jesus and died lost and the other who received Christ Jesus and was saved.

- **Satan was conquered.** In Genesis 3:15, God the Father promised, *"And I will put enmity between thee and the woman, and between thy seed and her seed; it shall bruise thy head, and thou shalt bruise his heel."* In comparison, Hebrews 2:14 states, *"Forasmuch then as the children are partakers of flesh and blood, he also himself likewise took part of the same; that through death he might destroy him that had the power of death, that is, the devil."* From these two Scriptures, we learn that at a place called Calvary, Jesus Christ conquered sin, death, and satanic principalities in the heavenly places. In other words, Jesus Christ's shed blood, death, and resurrection brought victory over all spiritual forces of darkness.

Chapter 5
AT THE CROSS

෯

Our fundamental understanding continues with our gratitude for what occurred at the cross. Now that we understand the ramifications of what Jesus Christ won for us before Calvary and a place called Calvary, let us examine the cross itself.

> *And when they were come to the place, which is called Calvary, there they crucified him, and the malefactors, one on the right hand, and the other on the left* (Luke 23:33).

> *But God forbid that I should glory, save in the cross of our Lord Jesus Christ, by whom the world is crucified unto me, and I unto the world* (Gal. 6:14).

The blood of Jesus Christ never loses its power, and we can never comprehend the significance of Jesus Christ's shed blood without examining the cross. John 19:17 tells us this about our Savior, Jesus Christ:

And he bearing his cross went forth into a place called the place of a skull, which is called in the Hebrew Golgotha.

The cross is more than something to wear around your neck or a sign of your faith. The significance of the cross is not in its design, construction, or purpose but in its symbolic meaning of Jesus Christ's death.

Put it into your spirit that every time you see a cross, remember without fail what it really was: an instrument of a horrendous execution. Then recollect Jesus Christ's suffering upon the cross and profusely thank Him for His willingness to endure crucifixion so Jehovah God would forgive us for our sins.

The song "The Power of the Cross," sung by Keith and Kristyn Getty (Getty, Keith & Kristyn. "The Power of the Cross." Produced by John Schreiner. *Album In Christ Alone*) is a good rendition of the gratitude we should have for the cross.

The Power of the Cross
Oh, to see the dawn
Of the darkest day:
Christ on the road to Calvary
Tried by sinful men
Torn and beaten, then
Nailed to a cross of wood
This, the pow'r of the cross:
Christ became sin for us;
Took the blame, bore the wrath

We stand forgiven at the cross
Oh, to see the pain
Written on Your face
Bearing the awesome weight of sin
Ev'ry bitter thought
Ev'ry evil deed
Crowning Your bloodstained brow
Now the daylight flees;
Now the ground beneath
Quakes as its Maker bows His head
Curtain torn in two
Dead are raised to life;
"Finished!" the vict'ry cry

March Toward the Cross

Everything Jesus Christ did from the moment the Holy Spirit impregnated Mary was a march toward the cross. Christ Jesus knew and understood His destiny with the cross. Subsequently, that is why He became obedient unto death, even the death of the cross, to bear the sins of all men.[18]

Looking unto Jesus the author and finisher of
our faith; who for the joy that was set before
him endured the cross, despising the shame,

---

[18] Philippians 2:8 and 1 Peter 2:24

*and is set down at the right hand of the throne
of God* (Heb. 12:2).

Jesus Christ endured the momentary pain of the cross for
the joy that was set before Him. You may ask, what was the
joy set before Jesus Christ? Jesus Christ pursued the joy of
our redemption and salvation. Our Lord Jesus Christ traded
in short-term-intense suffering for the long-term intense joy
of redeeming mankind and doing His Father's will.

It is at the cross that Jesus Christ built a divine bridge
between heaven and earth with three nails and two boards. It
is at the cross where Jesus Christ became the way for humanity
to pass from the degradation of sin to the glory of heaven. It is
at the cross Jesus Christ made it possible to go from rejection
to redemption. It is at the cross that we must also remember
the cross is a place of intersection—a meeting place if you
will. Let us examine this meeting place and what intersected/
happened there.

Great Exchange Provided by Jesus Christ

- It is at the cross Jesus Christ offered us the most amazing
  deal in eternity:

- Our sin for His righteousness

> *For he hath made him to be sin for us, who knew no sin; that we might be made the righteousness of God in him* (2 Cor. 5:21).

- Our weakness for His strength so that the power of Jesus Christ rests upon us

> *And he said unto me, My grace is sufficient for thee: for my strength is made perfect in weakness. Most gladly therefore will I rather glory in my infirmities, that the power of Christ may rest upon me* (2 Cor. 12:9).

- Our poverty for His riches

> *But thou shalt remember the Lord thy God: for it is he that giveth thee power to get wealth, that he may establish his covenant which he sware unto thy fathers, as it is this day* (Deut. 8:18).

> *But my God shall supply all your need according to his riches in glory by Christ Jesus* (Phil. 4:19).

- Our sickness for His health

> *Surely he hath borne our griefs, and carried our sorrows: yet we did esteem him stricken, smitten of God, and afflicted. But he was wounded*

*for our transgressions, he was bruised for our
iniquities: the chastisement of our peace was
upon him; and with his stripes we are healed*
(Isa. 53:4–5).

*Beloved, I wish above all things that thou
mayest prosper and be in health, even as thy
soul prospereth* (3 John 2).

Best of God

At the cross, the best of God stood waiting for mankind, and the worst of mankind met the best of God. It was at the cross that Jesus Christ drenched us with His blood and mankind came from this meeting with the best of God poured out on mankind—*blood-drenched, blood-bought, blood-stained, and blood-washed.*

Divine Love Met Sinful Mankind

The cross is the intersection of God's wrath, holiness, and divine love meeting sinful mankind. At the meeting place, God bestowed His mercy and love on an undeserving population—humanity.

Jesus Christ Destroyed the Works of the Devil

It is at the cross that Jesus Christ destroyed the twenty-five works of the devil.[19]

1. Sin-rebellion (Genesis 3:2, 2 Cor. 11:3)
2. Works of darkness, including moral sedition and sex perversion (Eph. 5:11; 6:12, Acts 16:18)
3. Works of wickedness (Col. 1:21)
4. Spiritual blindness (2 Cor. 4:4)
5. Stealing the Word of God (Matt. 13:19)
6. Deceptions and false religions (2 Cor. 11:14, 1 Tim. 4; Rev. 12:9)
7. To kill and destroy (John 10:10)
8. Sowing tares, tempting, and sifting saints (Matt. 4:3; 13:25; Luke 22:31)
9. Promoting counterfeit worship and miracles (2 Thess. 2:8–12; 1 Cor. 10:20)
10. Causing storms (Job 1:18–19; Eph. 2:2)
11. Ruling nations (Matt. 4:8–9; Dan. 10)
12. Executing death (Heb. 2:14–15)
13. Accusing the brethren (Rev. 12:10)
14. Hindering prayers (Dan. 10:12–21)
15. Opposing the gospel (Eph. 6:1–18)
16. Supervising demons (John 12:31), fallen angels (Rev. 12:7–12), and fallen man (Eph. 2:2; 1 John 3:8; John 8:44)

---

[19] Dake, Finis, Jennings, *Dake's Annotated Reference Bible* (Ninth Printing edition), (Lawrenceville: Dake Publishing, Inc, 2006), 484 and 489, note x.

17. Causing sickness and disease (Matt. 4:23–24; 9:32–33; 15:22; Acts 10:38)
18. Causing infirmities (Matt. 8:17; Luke 13:16; John 10:10; Acts 10:38)
19. Causing lunacy and mania (Matt. 4:23–24; 17:14–21; Mark 5:1–18)
20. Urging suicides (Matt. 17:15; John 10:10)
21. Agitating lusts (John 8:44; Eph. 2:1–3)
22. Lying and false prophecy (1 Kings 22; Matt. 24:2, 11; 2 Cor. 11:13–15)
23. Propagating false doctrines (1 Tim. 4:2; 2 Tim. 4; 2 Thess. 2; Rev. 13)
24. Oppressing men (Acts 10:38)
25. Persecuting Christians and warring on saints (Eph. 6:10–18; 1 Pet. 5:8–9)

> *He that committeth sin is of the devil; for the devil sinneth from the beginning. For this purpose the Son of God was manifested, that he might destroy the works of the devil* (1 John 3:8).

Jesus Christ Became Our Sins

Christ Jesus's soul was made an offering for our sins as a complete substitute and sacrifice for mankind. "*He bore our sins in His own body on the tree, that we, being dead to sins, should live unto righteousness.*"[20]

It is imperative that we understand what happened when Jesus Christ bore our sins.

First, it is extremely important to understand that God hates sin. God cannot let evil abide in His presence, so He pronounced a death sentence on sinners.

> *For the wages of sin is death; but the gift of God*
> *is eternal life through Jesus Christ our Lord*
> (Rom. 6:23).

However, 1 John 4:8 clearly tells us that God is love, and He created us, intending to care for us. In fact, the Lord desires that all people spend eternity with Him. Yet there remains the problem of our sin and the penalty that we owe.

The Lord cannot violate His own nature. Though God loves mankind, His holiness would be compromised if He permitted the filth of sin into His presence. So, the Father made a way to cleanse dirty hearts and transform wayward natures. He put the sin of all mankind on Jesus Christ's shoulders!

We must unmistakably grasp this concept, especially what it did to Jesus Christ who *"did no sin, neither was guile found*

---

[20] 1 Peter 2:24; compare 2 Corinthians 5:21

in his mouth."[21] In Matthew 26:39, Jesus Christ asked the Father not to let Him drink of this cup:

And he went a little farther, and fell on his face, and prayed, saying, O my Father, if it be possible, let this cup pass from me: nevertheless not as I will, but as thou wilt.

You may wonder why Jesus Christ, who knew and understood His destiny with the cross, asked this of the Father. At the moment Jesus Christ drank of the cup, a cup containing the filth of sin, He became sin for us. Since sin cannot exist in the presence of God and God cannot change His holy nature, consequently, for the first time in eternity, God the Father had to separate Himself from Jesus Christ, who now carried all the sins of mankind. As a result, we see Jesus Christ at the cross crying out.

> *And about the ninth hour Jesus cried with a loud voice, saying, Eli, Eli, lama sabachthani? that is to say, My God, my God, why hast thou forsaken me* (Matt. 27:46)?

Imagine the grueling anxiety this momentary separation from God the Father caused Jesus Christ as God passed judgment on sin. Jesus Christ, at the lowest point of His suffering, now experienced the full brunt of His Father's wrath, which spared you and me from this fate!

---

[21] 1 Peter 2:22

In His cry, Jesus Christ expressed the agony of unbearable stress and the hellish cry uttered when the undiluted wrath of God overwhelms the soul. The cry, *"My God, my God, why hast thou forsaken me?"* is heart-piercing, heaven-piercing, and hell-piercing—the expressed agony of unmitigated sin. All the sins of humanity and the hell that we deserve for eternity were laid upon our faithful Lord Jesus Christ.

In His hour of greatest need came a pain unlike anything Jesus Christ, the Son, had ever experienced, His Father's abandonment and separation. Every detail of this horrific separation from the Father declares the heinous character of our sins!

Fortunately for us, with Jesus Christ as our substitute, God's wrath is satisfied, and He can justify those who believe in His Son, Jesus Christ. Jesus Christ's penal suffering, therefore, is vicarious—He suffered on our behalf. Jesus Christ did not simply share our forsakenness but saved us from it! Jesus Christ endured it for us, not with us.

Unfortunately, sometimes believers, especially those who have known Jesus Christ for a long time, are inclined to forget what their sin cost our Savior, the Lord Jesus Christ. It behooves us to remember how Jesus Christ suffered for our sake. For example, Jesus Christ suffered:

- **Physical pain.** Before His crucifixion, Jesus Christ was mocked, beaten, humiliated, and then nailed to the cross to endure an excruciating death.

- **Man's sin.** Jesus Christ bore our sins in His own body on the tree, that we, being dead to sins, should live unto righteousness. Also, He experienced the fullness of our transgressions, along with the guilt, shame, and regret.

  > *For he hath made him to be sin for us, who knew no sin; that we might be made the righteousness of God in him* (2 Cor. 5:21).

  > *Who his own self bare our sins in his own body on the tree, that we, being dead to sins, should live unto righteousness: by whose stripes ye were healed* (1 Pet. 2:24).

- **Abandonment.** For the first time in eternity, God the Father had to separate Himself from Jesus Christ, who now carried all the sins of mankind. As a result, we see Jesus Christ at the cross crying out, *"My God, my God, why hast thou forsaken me?"*

- **Divine Judgment.** Jesus Christ, at the lowest point of His suffering, experienced the full brunt of His Father's wrath, which spared you and me from this fate! Jesus Christ experienced the condemnation we rightly deserved.

We are immune to condemnation and the curse of the law because we are in Christ Jesus, and He bore it for us in that outer darkness. Golgotha secured our immunity, not mere sympathy.

> *There is therefore now no condemnation to them which are in Christ Jesus, who walk not after the flesh, but after the Spirit* (Rom. 8:1).

> *To declare, I say, at this time his righteousness: that he might be just, and the justifier of him which believeth in Jesus* (Rom. 3:26).

> *Christ hath redeemed us from the curse of the law, being made a curse for us: for it is written, Cursed is every one that hangeth on a tree* (Gal. 3:13).

Apostle Paul's teachings in Romans further enhance our understanding of immunity to condemnation. For example, he teaches believers are not only free from bondage to sin, but they are also free from the inner emotions and thoughts that tend to bring feelings of condemnation to the Christian when the person does commit sin.

> *For the law of the Spirit of life in Christ Jesus hath made me free from the law of sin and death* (Rom. 8:2).

Paul further teaches that Christians are free from the "law of sin and death," which means, although they will commit sin, the law does not any longer has the power to condemn them. He also teaches we are not under the law's condemnation because Jesus Christ fulfilled ("filled-up, completed." https://www.gotquestions.org/abolish-fulfill-law.html) the expectations of the law perfectly, and believers are "in Christ."

> *For what the law could not do, in that it was weak through the flesh, God sending his own Son in the likeness of sinful flesh, and for sin, condemned sin in the flesh: That the righteousness of the law might be fulfilled in us, who walk not after the flesh, but after the Spirit* (Rom. 8:3–4).

Since believers are in Jesus Christ, they have the joy of being counted as righteous simply because Jesus Christ is righteous (Phil. 3:9). Apostle Paul also points out that genuine Christians, although they struggle, will not live "according to the flesh," that is, they will not persist in a constant state of sinful living.

> *For they that are after the flesh do mind the things of the flesh; but they that are after the Spirit the things of the Spirit* (Rom. 8:5).

Before we continue with Apostle Paul's teaching, let us explore what does it mean Christians will not persist in a constant state of sinful living? Just because we as Christians have immunity to condemnation because of Jesus Christ does not give us a license to sin. An examination of the below passage is needed to understand this concept.

> *Whosoever is born of God doth not commit sin;*
> *for his seed remaineth in him: and he cannot*
> *sin, because he is born of God* (1 John 3:9).

In this verse, the emphasis is on the one "born of God." Apostle John's advice to us as Christians is that this does not mean a believer can willfully live a life of depravity, and there is not an excuse for sin in the life of a believer. God's gracious acceptance is a motivation for holy obedience, and His grace is not a license to sin.

> *What shall we say then? Shall we continue in*
> *sin, that grace may abound* (Rom. 6:1)?

The Godhead dwells bodily in the believer and because *"greater is He that is in you, than he that is in the world"* (1 John 4:4), the believer cannot any longer live the same life as prior to becoming God's child. Though believers continue to sin, we are changed more into the likeness of Jesus Christ.

We must confess our sins and come to a place where we willingly acknowledge our wrongdoing and ask God for forgiveness. Once we do this, God will forgive us! We are cleansed from all sin from the time of confession of sin and as long as we walk in the light!

It is especially noteworthy to understand that if we claim we experience a shared life with Jesus Christ and continue to stumble around in the dark, we are obviously lying and do not know the truth—we are not living what we claim. Additionally, if we claim that we have never sinned, we out-and-out contradict God—make a liar out of Him. A claim like that only shows off our ignorance of God. However, when we walk in the light, God Himself being the light, we also experience a shared life with one another, as the sacrificed blood of Jesus Christ cleanses all our sins.

> *If we say that we have fellowship with him, and walk in darkness, we lie, and do not the truth* (1 John 1:6).

> *But if we walk in the light, as he is in the light, we have fellowship one with another, and the blood of Jesus Christ his Son cleanseth us from all sin* (1 John 1:7).

> *If we say that we have no sin, we deceive ourselves, and the truth is not in us* (1 John 1:8).

> *If we confess our sins, he is faithful and just to forgive us our sins, and to cleanse us from all unrighteousness* (1 John 1:9).

The devil wants us to believe that this is all a joke and that God may not want to forgive us anyway. However, Scripture clearly says God is faithful to do what He has promised, and He will forgive anyone who confesses.

> *Let us hold fast the profession of our faith without wavering; (for he is faithful that promised* (Heb. 10:23).

God will not only forgive our sins but will also cleanse us! If we consider a nail in a board as representing our sin, we would receive forgiveness when that nail was removed from the board, but a hole still remains. The cleansing God offers is like going back and filling the hole made by the nail. While cleansing from unrighteousness does not eliminate sin's consequences, it does more than just remove it. It removes the residue sin causes. It cleanses the conscience. Confession, forgiveness, and cleansing offer complete restoration to our life.[22]

Acts 26:18 informs us that not only does God forgives our sins, regardless of what we have done or who we hurt, but when we acknowledge we were wrong, repent of our sins,

---

[22] *Life Lights, Plan 2, Scripture 4 Note*, Hayford, Jack, *Spirit Filled Life Bible for Students*, New King James Version, (Nashville: Thomas Nelson Publishers, 1982), 1644.

and submit to God, He sets in motion a plan for us to get back on track.

> *To open their eyes, and to turn them from darkness to light, and from the power of Satan unto God, that they may receive forgiveness of sins, and inheritance among them which are sanctified by faith that is in me* (Acts 26:18).

God lovingly picks up the broken pieces of your life, and with the glue of His great love and forgiveness, God puts you back together and gives you a wonderful purpose.

Paul, in his defense at his trial before King Agrippa, used Acts 26:18 to illustrate the futility of his murderous mission in seeking to destroy Christianity, for his fight was against God, and the target of his abuse was the Lord Jesus Christ, the Son of God! During his trial, Paul recounted his background as a zealous persecutor of Christians and related his wonderful conversion. Paul mentioned that as he came near Damascus, suddenly there shined about him a light from heaven. He fell to the earth and heard a voice saying unto him, *"Saul, Saul, why persecutest thou me?"* The voice identified Himself as Jesus Christ and said, *"I am Jesus whom thou persecutest: it is hard for thee to kick against the pricks."*[23]

Despite Paul's blasphemy against God and his persecution of the body of Christ, God showed Paul mercy and grace

---

[23] Acts 9:3–9

without measure, and this visitation became a commission for Paul to participate in God's plan and purpose to proclaim the glorious gospel of Jesus Christ.

However, if we claim that we're free of sin, we're only fooling ourselves. Additionally, as previously mentioned, if we claim that we have never sinned, we out-and-out contradict God—make a liar out of Him.

> *If we say that we have no sin, we deceive ourselves, and the truth is not in us* (1 John 1:8).
>
> *If we say that we have not sinned, we make him a liar, and his word is not in us* (1 John 1:10).
>
> *Whosoever committeth sin transgresseth also the law: for sin is the transgression of the law. And ye know that he was manifested to take away our sins; and in him is no sin. Whosoever abideth in him sinneth not: whosoever sinneth hath not seen him, neither known him. Little children, let no man deceive you: he that doeth righteousness is righteous, even as he is righteous. He that committeth sin is of the devil; for the devil sinneth from the beginning. For this purpose the Son of God was manifested, that he might destroy the works of the devil. Whosoever is born of God doth not commit sin; for his seed*

> *remaineth in him: and he cannot sin, because*
> *he is born of God* (1 John 3:4–9).

We need to realize the meaning of 1 John 3:4–9. All who indulge in a sinful life are dangerously lawless, for sin is a major disruption of God's order.

Surely you know Jesus Christ came to rid us of sin. There is not any sin in Jesus Christ or part of His program. Not anyone who lives deeply in Jesus Christ makes a practice of sin. None of those who practice sin have taken a good look at Jesus Christ. They've got Jesus Christ all backward. Those who make a practice of continuous sin are straight from Satan, the pioneer in the practice of sin. This is why the Son of God, our Lord and Savior, Jesus Christ, entered the world to abolish the devil's ways. Praise be to God.

People conceived and brought into life by God don't make a practice of sin. How could they? It's not in the nature of the God-born to practice and parade sin. God's seed is deep within them, making them who they are.

Here's a simple test on how you can tell the difference between God's children and the devil's children. The one who won't practice righteous ways isn't from God, nor is the one who won't love his brother or sister.

As Christians, we must become dead to sin and alive to God. "*For sin shall not have dominion over you: for ye are not under the law, but under grace*" (Rom. 6:14). We need to turn off the sin switch, as Paul states in Romans 6:11–22. In these verses, Paul revealed a great secret in the Christian life because of Jesus Christ's power in our lives, we are not any longer have to be slaves to sin. In other words, when temptations and desires to disobey God crop up in our lives, we not any longer have to give in to those desires.

God has now given us Jesus Christ's power at work in us to turn off the sin switch and turn on the righteousness switch. We still have the power to choose which switch we want to turn on or off. But if we choose to turn on the righteousness switch, the power to live holy and pure lives will flood into our being.[24]

Additionally, Apostle Paul encourages us that we need not fear condemnation and guilt because we can come to God, our loving, forgiving Father.

> *There is therefore now no condemnation to them which are in Christ Jesus, who walk not after the flesh, but after the Spirit* (Rom. 8:1).

> *For ye have not received the spirit of bondage again to fear; but ye have received the Spirit of adoption, whereby we cry, Abba, Father. The Spirit itself beareth witness with our spirit, that we are the children of God* (Rom. 8:15–16).

---

[24] *Turn Off the Sin Switch Note*, Hayford, Jack, *Spirit Filled Life Bible for Students,* New King James Version, (Nashville: Thomas Nelson Publishers, 1982), 1455.

Unfortunately, many people struggle because they feel guilt over past sins, such as stealing, adultery, fornication, idolatry, witchcraft, hatred, and drunkenness, and believe God will not hear their prayers. The cure if guilt remains after confessing your sins, stand upon the Word of God. We must fully understand God is satisfied with the blood of Jesus Christ as payment for our sins. When Jesus Christ went to the cross for us, He lifted the guilt as well as the penalty for sin from our shoulders and made us righteous. His precious blood wiped our sins clean, but guilt may plague us because the sins we commit stain our conscience.

A guilty conscience is a serious matter. It is simply amazing how the blood of Jesus Christ, which requires God to forgive us, obliterates the stain and purifies our conscience. That is how powerful the blood of Jesus Christ is! God waits with open arms, unconditional love, and forgiveness for us to approach Him—always willing to set us back on the right course.[25] Subsequently, in Philippians 3:13, Paul encourages Christians who live in shame and guilt over past failures to needlessly condemn themselves when they ought to forget those things that are behind and reach toward what is ahead.

Fear is paralyzing, *"but perfect love drives out fear"* (1 John 4:18). As Christians, we must understand our justification is found in Jesus Christ alone in His finished work on the cross, not in what we do or do not do. Believers can find solace in the assurance that God adopted us into His own family and

---

[25] *Sustained Under Pressure*, Stanley, Charles F, *God's Purpose for Your Life*, (Nashville: Thomas Nelson Publishers, 2020), 251.

made us heirs of God and co-heirs with Jesus Christ. Nothing can separate us *"from the love of God which is in Christ Jesus."*

> *Therefore we conclude that a man is justified by faith without the deeds of the law* (Rom. 3:28).

> *And if children, then heirs; heirs of God, and joint-heirs with Christ; if so be that we suffer with him, that we may be also glorified together* (Rom. 8:17).

> *Nor height, nor depth, nor any other creature, shall be able to separate us from the love of God, which is in Christ Jesus our Lord* (Rom. 8:39).

When Satan tries to remind you of your past, remind him of his future. He will be thrown into the lake of fire for all eternity.

> *And the devil that deceived them was cast into the lake of fire and brimstone, where the beast and the false prophet are, and shall be tormented day and night for ever and ever* (Rev. 20:10).

CHAPTER 6

THE DIFFERENCE BETWEEN DRENCHED AND SPRINKLED IN THE BLOOD OF JESUS CHRIST

O ur fundamental understanding continues with our realization there is a tremendous difference between drenched and sprinkled in the blood of Jesus Christ.

In short, *drenched* means completely soaked/saturated[26]. Whereas, *sprinkled* means to scatter or slightly drizzle in small measures[27]. God wants to completely soak/saturate us with the blood of Jesus Christ until the Spirit, without measure, oozes through us with the power, authority, and strength of the Godhead that dwells bodily in us. To receive the Spirit

---

[26] https://biblehub.com/topical/d/drench.htm

[27] Strong's #2236 zaraq zaw-rak' a primitive root; to sprinkle (fluid or solid particles): —be here and there, scatter, sprinkle, strew

without measure means we can do all the works of our Lord Jesus Christ and even greater works than He did.

> *For he whom God hath sent speaketh the words of God: for God giveth not the Spirit by measure unto him* (John 3:34).

> *In the last day, that great day of the feast, Jesus stood and cried, saying, If any man thirst, let him come unto me, and drink. He that believeth on me, as the scripture hath said, out of his belly shall flow rivers of living water* (John 7:37–38).

> *For in him dwelleth all the fulness of the Godhead bodily* (Col. 2:9).

On the other hand, as noted in Hebrews 9:13;12:24, and 1 Peter 1:2, we are sprinkled with the blood of Jesus Christ to purge our conscience from sin, wash our souls, and make us inwardly holy before God. Put another way, the *"blood of sprinkling"* (Heb. 12:24) represents the pains, sufferings, humiliation, and ultimate death of our Lord and Savior Jesus Christ, which He endured on behalf of the guilty man.

> *For if the blood of bulls and of goats, and the ashes of an heifer sprinkling the unclean, sanctifieth to the purifying of the flesh* (Heb. 9:13).

> *And to Jesus the mediator of the new covenant,*
> *and to the blood of sprinkling, that speaketh*
> *better things than that of Abel* (Heb. 12:24).

> *Elect according to the foreknowledge of God*
> *the Father, through sanctification of the Spirit,*
> *unto obedience and sprinkling of the blood of*
> *Jesus Christ: Grace unto you, and peace, be*
> *multiplied* (1 Pet. 1:2).

Through the sprinkling of Jesus Christ's blood, we become God's elect. This takes place at the moment we receive salvation. The blood of sprinkling is only a measure of the fullness of the power, authority, might, and strength God wants to bestow upon our lives, whereas drenched in the blood of Jesus Christ through the Spirit is without measure and essential for spiritual warfare engagement.

We need to fully understand when Jesus Christ drenches us in His blood, it baptizes us into the power, authority, might, and strength of His Holy Spirit. The blood of Jesus Christ never loses its power and is inexhaustible. Being drenched in the blood of Jesus Christ gives us power, authority, might, and strength to engage in spiritual warfare boldly, fully, and effectively.

Ephesians 6:12 tells us that we wrestle not against flesh and blood but against Satan and his demonic forces. The blood of Jesus Christ is a mighty effective armament for our arsenal of spiritual weapons. That is why being drenched in the blood of Jesus Christ and, most importantly, knowing that you are drenched, walking in that drenching, and welding the drenching as a weapon cause you to stand and demonic forces to coward in fear, knowing that they cannot withstand the onslaught of the power, authority, might, and strength flowing from the blood of Jesus Christ.

> *For we wrestle not against flesh and blood, but against principalities, against powers, against the rulers of the darkness of this world, against spiritual wickedness in high places. (Wherefore take unto you the whole armour of God, that ye may be able to withstand in the evil day, and having done all, to stand* (Eph. 6:12–13).

Accept and Walk in the Drenching. You are drenched in the blood of Jesus Christ. You must know this without a shadow of a doubt. Lock this in your soul, get it deep in your spirit, live it, walk in it, open your mouth, and confess it. Allow these words, *"I am drenched in the blood of Jesus Christ,"* to grow and take root in your heart and your soul and bind them for a sign upon your hand that they may be as frontlets between your eyes.

Absorb the Drenching. You are drenched in the blood of Jesus Christ. You must become acutely conscious of this and absorb it in your spirit. Jesus Christ drenches you in His blood so that you become powerfully attuned to your God-given authority over Satan, demons, and the host of demonic forces through the precious blood of Jesus Christ.

Tap Into and Flow in the Drenching. You are drenched in the blood of Jesus Christ. Tap into and flow in the drenching. Realize there's an anointing born out of adversity that throws off anything hell sends your way. Never give up and refuse to die in the midst of spiritual warfare but live and declare the works of the Lord. From henceforth, do not let demonic forces trouble you. Always remember you are drenched in the blood of Jesus Christ and bear in your body the marks of our Lord Jesus Christ.

Power, Strength, and Might of the Drenching. You are drenched in the blood of Jesus Christ. Jesus Christ drenches you in His blood to gird you with power, strength, and might of His Holy Spirit to make your name known before your adversaries so that they may tremble at your very presence. This is why Satan, demons, and the host of demonic forces will do everything possible to keep you distracted, send people or ideas to confuse you, or plant seeds of doubt to hide the truth to ensure you are not aware and ignorant of the fact that you are drenched in the blood of Jesus Christ.

See Yourself in the Drenching. You are drenched in the blood of Jesus Christ. Create this image and see yourself drenched in the blood of Jesus Christ. Once the drenching becomes real internally, it then manifests externally. Subsequently, the words that come out of your mouth will align/agree with the drenching power of the blood of Jesus Christ.

Hear ye this day, this moment in eternity, God wants to bring you to a place of total drenching, a complete soaking and thorough saturating, where He thoroughly washes you from head to toe in the blood of Jesus Christ and drenches you to the point where you are saturated with the blood of Jesus Christ, where you are wet through and through with the blood of Jesus Christ, and where you see, smell, taste, and walk in the blood of Jesus Christ. Stand ready for the drenching so that you come to realize, *I Am Drenched in the Blood of Jesus Christ, Blood Bought, Blood Stained, Blood Washed.*

> *O' Heavenly Father Drench Me Through*
> *and Through*
> *O' Heavenly Father, drench me through*
> *and through.*
> *O' the blood of the Lamb, how precious is*
> *the blood.*
> *Drench me through and through.*
> *How I need a drenching from You.*
> *O' Heavenly Father, drench me through*
> *and through.*
> *I lift up holy arms to receive a*
> *drenching from You.*
> *O' Heavenly Father, drench me through*
> *and through.*
> *Every step I take is blood bought, blood*
> *stained, and blood washed.*

O' Heavenly Father, drench me through
and through.
I need the drenching now.
O' Heavenly Father, drench me through
and through.
I am drenched in the blood of Jesus Christ.
O' Heavenly Father, drench me through
and through;
Blood bought, blood stained, and
blood washed.

CHAPTER 7
I AM DRENCHED IN THE BLOOD OF JESUS CHRIST BLOOD BOUGHT

᠀

Forasmuch as ye know that ye were not redeemed with corruptible things, as silver and gold, from your vain conversation received by tradition from your fathers; But with the precious blood of Christ, as of a lamb without blemish and without spot (1 Pet. 1:18–19).

For ye are bought with a price: therefore glorify God in your body, and in your spirit, which are God's (1 Cor. 6:20).

We can only fully understand what drenched in the blood of Jesus Christ is by comprehending we are *Blood Bought, Blood Stained, and Blood Washed.* This chapter examines the first aspect: *Blood Bought.*

1 Corinthians 6:20 is critical to our understanding that we were bought with a price. That price is the precious blood of Jesus Christ. We routinely sing the song "There Is Power in the Blood." The refrain of this song boldly declares how precious is the blood of Jesus Christ. ("There Is Power in the Blood" sung by Lewis E. Jones)[28].

> *There is pow'r, pow'r, wonder-working pow'r*
> *In the blood of the Lamb;*
> *There is pow'r, pow'r, wonder-working pow'r*
> *In the precious blood of the Lamb.*

Vital to our blood-bought understanding is that the Almighty God redeemed each of us with the precious blood of Christ, as of a lamb without blemish or spot. The blood of Jesus Christ is more precious than any other means and fulfills our deepest aches and longings in God, not just temporarily but finally and forever.

Jesus Christ willingly offered Himself as the sacrificial Lamb of God, shedding His own blood, once and for all. At the moment Jesus Christ shed His precious blood, He saved us from the consequence of sin. How did He do this? Jesus Christ gave Himself to bear the punishment due to our sin in His own body on the cross so that we, being dead to sins, should live unto righteousness. This means Jesus Christ

---

[28] Jones, Lewis E, *There Is Power In the Blood, (*Guthrie: Faith Publishing House, Evening Light Songs, 1949, edited 1987), https://library.timelesstruths.org/music/There_Is_Power_in_the_Blood/.

became our propitiation or covering for sin. In essence, Jesus Christ bought us with His blood so that we could experience the eight blood-bought benefits listed below.

1. Forgiveness: to restore our relationship with the Father
2. Justification: to extend God's full acceptance
3. Pacification: to make peace with the Father
4. Propitiation (covering for sin): to remove God's righteous wrath
5. Reconciliation: to make sinners one with the Father
6. Redemption: to purchase our true freedom
7. Salvation: to save, deliver, and redeem
8. Sanctification: to set apart/separate unto God through Jesus Christ's blood

Forgiveness: To Restore Our Relationship with the Father

> *For thou, Lord, art good, and ready to forgive; and plenteous in mercy unto all them that call upon thee* (Ps. 86:5).

> *And forgive us our debts, as we forgive our debtors* (Matt. 6:12).

God graciously forgives us because a relationship in the right standing is of the utmost importance to God, our Father, and we see this in being blood-bought.

God commands goodness and mercy to follow us all the days of our life for us to experience His kindness and dwell in the right relationship with Him in the house of the Lord forever. Essentially, God demonstrates His kindness, goodness, and mercy toward us by not leaving us in the condition of an unrighteous relationship that we existed in before salvation and when Jesus Christ's blood-bought us.

God's forgiveness entails three aspects:

1. God's Forgiveness: What's Required?

Hebrews 9:22 gives us the costly requirement for God's forgiveness, there is not any forgiveness without the shedding of blood.

And almost all things are by the law purged with blood; and without shedding of blood is no remission (Heb. 9:22).

In the Old Testament, we witness the continual sacrifices of unblemished lambs required to satisfy God's wrath and judgment. However, when Jesus Christ died on the cross as the Lamb of God, He purchased God's forgiveness and became the ultimate, once-and-for-all sacrifice for the sins of the righteous as well as the unrighteous to bring us to God.

In whom we have redemption through his blood, the forgiveness of sins, according to the riches of his grace (Eph. 1:7).

For Christ also hath once suffered for sins, the just for the unjust, that he might bring us to God, being put to death in the flesh, but quickened by the Spirit (1 Pet. 3:18).

2. God's Forgiveness: He Paid the Price Himself!

The price for God's forgiveness is high, but He paid the price Himself! Jesus Christ's loving act of grace eternally freed us from the penalty and guilt of sin. Once Jesus Christ has blood bought us, God does not keep a record of our sins. Our forgiveness is total and complete.

Blessed is he whose transgression is forgiven, whose sin is covered. Blessed is the man unto whom the Lord imputeth not iniquity, and in whose spirit there is no guile (Ps. 32:1–2).

3. God's Forgiveness: Once and for All!

A believer receives God's forgiveness when the believer repents sin and places faith in Jesus Christ for salvation, and God forgives all the believer's sins forever, including past, present, and future. Jesus Christ died to pay the penalty for all of our sins, and once they are forgiven, they are all forgiven. In fact, Scripture tell us that God, in His plenteous mercy, not only completely forgives our sins, but He also blots out our sins and remembers them not any longer. He does not rehash our sins to accuse us or punish us again and again.

Imagine if God chose not to include forgiveness in His holy plan to save and redeem us, then none of us would enjoy a renewed life and a right relationship with Him.

He hath not dealt with us after our sins; nor rewarded us according to our iniquities. For as the heaven is high above the earth, so great is his mercy toward them that fear him. As far as the east is from the west, so far hath he removed our transgressions from us (Ps. 103:10–12).

I, even I, am he that blotteth out thy transgressions for mine own sake, and will not remember thy sins (Isa. 43:25).

I have blotted out, as a thick cloud, thy transgressions, and, as a cloud, thy sins: return unto me; for I have redeemed thee (Isa. 44:22).

> *Repent ye therefore, and be converted, that your sins may be blotted out, when the times of refreshing shall come from the presence of the Lord* (Acts 3:19).

However, as mentioned before, when we stumble, we are called to confess our sins. We must confess and come to a place where we willingly acknowledge our wrongdoing and ask God for forgiveness. Once we do this, God will forgive us!

> *If we confess our sins, he is faithful and just to forgive us our sins, and to cleanse us from all unrighteousness* (1 John 1:9).

Justification: To Extend God's Full Acceptance

> *But God commendeth his love toward us, in that, while we were yet sinners, Christ died for us. Much more then, being now justified by his blood, we shall be saved from wrath through him* (Rom. 5:8–9).

Romans 5:9 says, "*we have now been justified by his blood.*" *Justified* is courtroom language. The prosecution and defense each present their case, and the judge or jury makes a declaration: either righteous or condemned. The defendant is either guilty as charged or declared to be in right standing with the law—justified. Be it known the blood of Jesus Christ is our defense, and God Himself declares us acceptable to Him and guilty not any longer. That is what the blood of Jesus Christ does for us.

Pacification: To Make Peace with the Father

That thou mayest remember, and be confounded, and never open thy mouth any more because of thy shame, when I am pacified toward thee for all that thou hast done, saith the Lord God (Ezek. 16:63).

For it pleased the Father that in him should all fulness dwell; And, having made peace through the blood of his cross, by him to reconcile all things unto himself; by him, I say, whether they be things in earth, or things in heaven (Col. 1:19–20).

We cannot make peace with the Father because our sinful nature stands in the way. But Almighty God made a way for us to experience peace with Him. Colossians 1:19–20 makes it clear when Jesus Christ bought us, His blood ultimately made peace between God and His people. Not only did Jesus Christ's blood make peace for us, but it also effectively reconciled us to the Almighty God.

Jesus Christ did not shed His precious blood by accident. This was not a random death. Tragic as it was, it was deliberate and voluntary. Jesus Christ laid down His life on our behalf so that we experience peace

> *No man taketh it from me, but I lay it down of myself. I have power to lay it down, and I have power to take it again. This commandment have I received of my Father* (John 10:18).

At the cross, Jesus Christ intentionally shed His blood so that we can encounter peace with God and let the peace of God rule in our hearts. Furthermore, in doing so, Jesus Christ not only blood bought our true freedom but, most importantly, restored our relationship and made peace for us with God. Simultaneously, Jesus Christ guaranteed our peace with God and unconstrained access by faith to our heavenly Father.

> *Therefore being justified by faith, we have peace with God through our Lord Jesus Christ: By whom also we have access by faith into this grace wherein we stand, and rejoice in hope of the glory of God* (Rom. 5:1–2).

> *And let the peace of God rule in your hearts, to the which also ye are called in one body; and be ye thankful* (Col. 3:15).

Propitiation (Covering for Sin): To Remove God's
Righteous Wrath

> *O death, where is thy sting? O grave, where is*
> *thy victory? The sting of death is sin; and the*
> *strength of sin is the law. But thanks be to God,*
> *which giveth us the victory through our Lord*
> *Jesus Christ* (1 Cor. 15:55–57).

Way back in the garden of Eden, the Lord established a
rule to protect His creation. Do not disobey Me. Sin is a very
serious matter in His eyes, and He determined it deserved
the death penalty. Yet ever since Adam and Eve's transgression, we've been bound to slip up because we're flawed human
beings. God knew that! So, to save us from the consequence
of sin, He sent His Son to die in our place. Jesus Christ fulfilled the law while taking our punishment.

> *Whom God hath set forth to be a propitiation*
> *through faith in his blood, to declare his righ-*
> *teousness for the remission of sins that are past,*
> *through the forbearance of God* (Rom. 3:25).

We further see in Romans 3:25 that God set forth Jesus
Christ as His sacrifice to be a propitiation or covering for sin
received through faith in Jesus Christ's blood. Almighty God,
due to His righteousness and justice, could not merely sweep
our sins away. We have all sinned and come short of the glory

of God. Especially note what Romans 6:23 says, *"For the wages of sin is death; but the gift of God is eternal life through Jesus Christ our Lord."* In other words, divine justice is under obligation to give sinners their wages of eternal death and not the gift of eternal life.

> *And this is the record, that God hath given to us eternal life, and this life is in his Son. He that hath the Son hath life; and he that hath not the Son of God hath not life* (1 John 5:11-12).

> *And this is life eternal, that they might know thee the only true God, and Jesus Christ, whom thou hast sent* (John 17:3).

However, our merciful Father lovingly acted to free us from the penalty of sin, satisfy justice, and still triumph with mercy. We need to recognize the price of sin is blood, in particular, the blood of Jesus Christ. This is why God commended His love toward us, in that, while we were yet sinners, Jesus Christ died for us and blood bought us with His precious blood. This compassionate act of God justified us by the blood of Jesus Christ and saved us from His righteous wrath through Jesus Christ.

> *But God commendeth his love toward us, in that, while we were yet sinners, Christ died for us* (Rom. 5:8).

Reconciliation: To Make Sinners One with the Father

> *For it pleased the Father that in him should all fulness dwell; And, having made peace For if while we were enemies we were reconciled to God through the death of His Son, much more, having been reconciled, we shall be saved by His life* (Rom. 5:10).

> *And all things are of God, who hath reconciled us to himself by Jesus Christ, and hath given to us the ministry of reconciliation; To wit, that God was in Christ, reconciling the world unto himself, not imputing their trespasses unto them; and hath committed unto us the word of reconciliation* (2 Cor. 5:18–19).

> *For it pleased the Father that in him should all fulness dwell; And, having made peace through the blood of his cross, by him to reconcile all things unto himself; by him, I say, whether they be things in earth, or things in heaven. And you, that were sometime alienated and enemies in your mind by wicked works, yet now hath he reconciled. In the body of his flesh through death, to present you holy and unblameable and unreproveable in his sight* (Col. 1:19-22).

Reconciliation and the removal of enmity is a matter of concern to God. Enmity between God and humans happened in the garden of Eden. At the very moment of Adam and Eve's transgression, it broke our relationship with God. However, God had a plan through the death of His Son, Jesus Christ, to remove enmity, change it to friendship, and reconcile us to Him.

Reconciliation brings about a change in the relationship between God and humankind and from enmity and fragmentation to harmony and fellowship with God. Therefore, Jesus Christ blood bought us so we would not any longer be enemies but reconciled to God in friendship. Further, He blood bought us to reconcile us unto Himself and not impute our trespasses unto us. In doing so, Jesus Christ presents us to the Father as unblameable and unreprovable in His sight. Subsequently, His blood made it possible for us to experience peace and not alienation from God as His enemies.

Redemption: To Purchase Our True Freedom

Forasmuch as ye know that ye were not redeemed with corruptible things, as silver and gold, from your vain conversation received by tradition from your fathers (1 Pet. 1:18).

In whom we have redemption through his blood, the forgiveness of sins, according to the riches of his grace (Eph. 1:7).

Ephesians 1:7 says, "*In him we have redemption through his blood, the forgiveness of our sins.*" To redeem means to buy back or secure the freedom of someone in bondage. (https://www.dictionary.com/browse/redeemed). Redemption is the price God paid to manifest His grace and adopt us as sons.

Because of our sins, we all were (or continue to be) in spiritual captivity. Our violations of God's law mean we deserve His wrath. But in Jesus Christ, by the shedding of His blood, which forgives our sins before God, He purchases our freedom from justice and the power of Satan. "*Having forgiven us all our trespasses, by canceling the record of debt that stood against us with its legal demands,*" through His self-offering at the cross, Jesus Christ "*disarmed the rulers and authorities and put them to open shame, triumphing over them in it*" (Col. 2:13–15).

The decisive weapon Satan, our adversary, had against us was unforgiven sin. However, when Jesus Christ shed His precious blood in our place to forgive our sins, He ultimately purchased our true freedom and freed us from captivity. Jesus Christ redeemed us from Satan and the record of debt and legal demands against us.

Salvation[29]: To Save, Deliver, and Redeem

You may have thought about what salvation is and even how God works this miracle in our lives. Salvation is one of the greatest themes that challenge the hearts and minds of humans. Salvation is not a trivial subject— it is a matter of life and death. Yet how difficult it is to comprehend God's grace that forgives all our sins every day and night, without preconditions, without works—that is what salvation is all about!

For mine eyes have seen thy salvation (Luke 2:30).

Neither is there salvation in any other: for there is none other name under heaven given among men, whereby we must be saved (Acts 4:12).

For I am not ashamed of the gospel of Christ: for it is the power of God unto salvation to every one that believeth; to the Jew first, and also to the Greek (Rom. 1:16).

For God hath not appointed us to wrath, but to obtain salvation by our Lord Jesus Christ,

---

[29] Strong's #4991: Salvation is translated from the Greek word σωτηρία <soteria> (pronounced so-tay-ree'-ah) feminine of a derivative of 4990 as (properly, abstract) noun; rescue or safety (physically or morally): —deliver, health, salvation, save, saving.

Who died for us, that, whether we wake or sleep,
we should live together with him
(1 Thess. 5:9–10).

For the grace of God that bringeth salvation
hath appeared to all men (Titus 2:11).

The above Scriptures describe and help us understand God's plan of salvation. We must first set our mind on this truth: God, our Father, is a planner! God does not react. He plans and knows what He is doing. God has it all planned out—to take care of you, not abandon you, and plans to give you the future you hope for.[30]

God did not set this world in motion to let chance or unchecked forces rule it. Nor did God create us to live without hope or purpose. He has a plan!

Think about how carefully God planned our salvation. God strategically unfolded His grand design to send Jesus Christ, our Savior, throughout the ages, through changes in kings and empires, and nothing impeded Him. Then the good news went from the empty tomb to the disciples and from person to person until God's gift of salvation reached you.

Biblical salvation is God's way of providing His people with deliverance from sin and spiritual death through repentance and faith in His Son, Jesus Christ. Salvation is all God's

---

[30] Jeremiah 29:11

ideas and work. All we do is trust God enough to let Him do it. Salvation is God's gift from start to finish!

Jesus Christ purchased our salvation with His precious blood on the cross. God's eternal nature is holiness and righteousness. God cannot merely overlook our sins—His love will not permit it. God must punish sin or contradict His own holiness.

Salvation is a gift from God Almighty! All we have to do is reach out and receive this gift that comes by the "grace of God," His unmerited favor toward us, through which he shows us His love regardless of our imperfections. Salvation is a gift, pure and simple, and one so great that we would never have been able to afford it on our own. All we have to do is accept it!

However, there are many people who feel they need to work for their salvation or that they will receive salvation because they are good. But this is not the case. Jesus Christ's death on the cross accomplished our salvation.[31]

Since all have sinned and come short of the glory of God, as stated in Romans 3:23, all must be saved. None is so good that the person need not be saved, and none is so bad that the person cannot be saved. Even the vilest of sinners can be saved from the wrath of God by the saving grace of Jesus Christ. God's salvation by grace freely and unconditionally covers all.

---

[31] *Life Lights, Plan 3, Scripture 5 Note*, Hayford, Jack. *Spirit Filled Life Bible for Students*, New King James Version, (Nashville: Thomas Nelson Publishers,1982), 1533.

Three key prepositions in Ephesians 2:8–10 distinctly tell us how to be saved.[32]

> *For by **grace** are ye saved **through faith**; and that not of yourselves: it is the gift of God: Not of works, lest any man should boast. For we are his workmanship, created in Christ Jesus **unto good works**, which God hath before ordained that we should walk in them* (Eph. 2:8–10, emphasis added).

1. Salvation is *"by grace."* Grace means God saves us apart from any merit of our own. Grace is the unmerited love and favor of God shown to sinners.

2. Salvation is *"through faith."* Not anyone is saved by good works. Salvation is a gift that is totally by grace and must be received totally by faith.

3. Salvation is "***unto good works.***" We are not saved by good works, but we are saved to do good works. God creates each of us through Christ Jesus to join Him in the work He does, the good work He readied for us to do. Good

---

[32] Rogers, Adrian, *God's Plan of Salvation,* LaHaye, Tim, *Prophecy Study Bible.* New King James Version, (Chattanooga: AMG Publishers, 2000), 1134.

works are not the root of our salvation but the fruits of salvation.

Salvation for the believer in Jesus Christ has a three-fold nature regarding its timing: a past, a present, and a future.

1. **Past Salvation**. We now have salvation and are saved from all sin. We are saved from what we deserve as sinners because Jesus Christ died for us and bore in His body the curse that sin merits (2 Cor. 5:21; Gal. 3:13; Eph. 2:8; 1 Thess. 1:10; 2 Tim. 1:9).

2. **Present Salvation**. We are saved from the despotism of sin because we abide in Jesus Christ and look to Him, who lives in the power of endless life and who, by the Holy Spirit, is able to work in us mightily so that we can work out our own salvation with fear and trembling (Rom. 5:9; Phil. 2:12; 2 Tim. 3:15; Titus 2:11–12; Heb. 2:3; 6:9; 7:25; 1 John 1:7).

3. **Future Salvation.** We will be saved from the disgrace of sin when Christ returns, hence we wait for Him as a Savior (Phil. 3:20).
    1. For this, we are kept, and for this, Jesus Christ will return (Rom. 13:11; 1 Thess. 5:9; Heb. 5:9; 9:28; 1 Pet. 1:5, 9, 13).

2. Additionally, Hebrews 2:3 not only establishes the truth that salvation is great but also demonstrates that salvation should not be neglected.

How shall we escape, if we neglect so great salvation; which at the first began to be spoken by the Lord, and was confirmed unto us by them that heard him (Heb. 2:3).

The gospel is the good news of God's grace to give forgiveness and eternal life. Great salvation shows us that we can be confident of our salvation, certain we are forgiven by God, and sure we are destined for heaven.

Sanctification[33]: To Set Apart/Separation Unto God through Jesus Christ's Blood

But we are bound to give thanks always to God for you, brethren beloved of the Lord, because God hath from the beginning chosen you to salvation through sanctification of the Spirit and belief of the truth (2 Thess. 2:13).

---

[33] Sanctification comes from the verb sanctify. Sanctify originates from the Greek word hagiazo. Strong's #37: hagiazo (pronounced hag-ee-ad'-zo) from forty; to make holy, i.e. (ceremonially) purify or consecrate; (mentally) to venerate: —hallow, be holy, sanctify.

> *By the which will we are sanctified through the offering of the body of Jesus Christ once for all* (Heb. 10:10).

> *Wherefore Jesus also, that he might sanctify the people with his own blood, suffered without the gate* (Heb. 13:12).

The doctrine of sanctification teaches us that sanctification[34] is God's will for our lives and souls. Sanctification means to set apart for holy use; a separation unto God through Jesus Christ's blood from a profane, secular, and carnal use to a sacred, religious, and spiritual use.

Sanctification is frequently mentioned in the Word of God. Sanctification is God's will for our lives and souls. It is a process set in motion when we follow the Lord Jesus Christ. Additionally, God uses the sanctification process to share His holiness and make us more like His Son, Jesus Christ, by purifying our hearts and minds through repentance and prayer.

Furthermore, the sanctification process is progressive as evident in the Scriptures, just to name a few, like Luke 9:23,

---

[34] The meaning of sanctification comes to us from the Greek word hagiasmos and its root word hagios from which such English words as sanctify, sanctification, sanctuary, sacred, holy, saint and holiness are translated. Literally translated, considering its context and various forms, hagios means to set apart or make holy, to separate from defilement, dedicate, hallow, to be essentially pure, or to put into a state corresponding to the nature of God. https://www.bibledoctrines.org/2020/the-doctrine-of-sanctification/

Acts 14:22, Romans 1:11, Hebrews 3:6, and Jude 20–24. We also see in the Scriptures that sanctification is progressive holiness and grows in purity, which takes a lifetime. There is a need for progressive sanctification beyond that of salvation! This is where Christian growth and maturity come in. It begins from the first moment we receive salvation through sanctification, as expressed in 2 Thessalonians 2:13, our spiritual birth when we put off the old man and put on the new man and to the last moment when Jesus Christ presents us faultless before the presence of God's glory with exceeding joy.

Throughout the progressive sanctification process, Jesus Christ is able to keep us from falling. Also, as expressed in John 14:26; 16:7-11, Jesus Christ sent the Comforter, the Holy Spirit, to aid us in sanctification, comfort us, help us overcome corruptions, restrain lust, increase our faith, inflame love and brighten hope.

Therefore, we can rightly conclude that God's ultimate aim is for us to be sanctified and grow in holiness, but unless we are regenerated or born again, we do not have any hope to be sanctified because sanctification takes the power of the Holy Spirit. It is impossible by human effort. Paul says that *"the sinful nature desires what is contrary to the Spirit and the Spirit what is contrary to the sinful nature. They are in conflict with each other, so that you do not do what you want"* (Gal. 5:17).

What is God's will for your life? To be sanctified and grow in holiness, for God says, *"Be holy because I, the LORD your God, am holy"* (Lev. 19:2). Paul knew this as he wrote, *"It is*

God's will that you should be sanctified: that you should avoid sexual immorality" (1 Thess. 4:3). This is exactly why *"he hath chosen us in him before the foundation of the world, that we should be holy and without blame before him in love"* (Eph. 1:4).

Eight Blood-Bought Benefits Summarized

In summary, Jesus Christ bought us with His blood so that we can experience the eight blood-bought benefits previously discussed:

1. Forgiveness: to restore our relationship with the Father
2. Justification: to extend God's full acceptance
3. Pacification: to make peace with the Father
4. Propitiation (covering for sin): to remove God's righteous wrath
5. Reconciliation: to make sinners one with the Father
6. Redemption: to purchase our true freedom
7. Salvation: to save, deliver, and redeem
8. Sanctification: to set apart/separation unto God through Jesus Christ's blood

Spiritual Blessings in Heavenly Places

In the same way, Jesus Christ bought us with His blood so that we can experience the eight blood-bought benefits when He blood-bought us, He also blessed us with all spiritual blessings in heavenly places in Jesus Christ.

Blessed be the God and Father of our Lord Jesus Christ, who hath blessed us[35] with all spiritual blessings in heavenly places in Christ (Eph. 1:3).

All spiritual blessings are reserved specifically for people who confess with their hearts the Lord Jesus Christ and believe in their hearts that God raised Him from the dead and reunited with Jesus Christ in faith. Furthermore, spiritual blessings characterize the key benefits of a relationship with God through Jesus Christ.

Ephesians 1:4–14 records nine spiritual blessings. Three are from the work of God the Father, four from the work of God the Son, Jesus Christ, and two from the work of the Holy Spirit, as summarized in the below table:

---

[35] The "us" includes both Jews and Gentiles in the church at Ephesus and beyond. It is important to point out that these blessings are for both Jewish and Gentile believers. Guzik, David. "God's Ultimate Plan." https://www.blueletterbible.org/Comm/archives/guzik_david/StudyGuide_Eph/Eph_1.cfm. (Accessed June 30, 2021)

God **Leave Past Behind**	Jesus Christ **Rejoice in the Present**	Holy Spirit **Confidence in the Future**
Chose us (v. 4)	Redeemed us (v. 7)	Sealed us (v. 13)
Adopted us (v. 5)	Forgave us (v. 7)	Gave us down payment of what's to come; guarantee our inheritance (v. 14)
Accepted us (v. 6)	Revealed God's will to us (vv. 9, 10)	
	Inheritance given to us (v. 11)	

Chose Us

The first spiritual blessing listed in verse 4 is God *chose us*—the election as saints. Eklegomai[36] is the Greek word for "to make a choice." *Election* occurs six times[37] in the New Testament. Election is unconditional in the sense that God did not base His choice on His foreknowledge of whether certain people would choose to believe in Jesus Christ. If He had done so, it would be a denial of His grace that God offers to everyone. His grace elects to save all who will believe. If it were not so, then individuals' salvation would be based on something they did in and of themselves and not of God. But Scripture is clear that salvation is totally by God's grace.

---

[36] Strong's #1586: ἐκλέγομαι eklégomai, ek-leg>-om-ahee; middle voice from G1537 and G3004 (in its primary sense); to select:—make choice, choose (out), chosen.

[37] Romans 9:11; 11:5,7,28; 1 Thessalonians 1:4; 2 Peter 1:10

For the children being not yet born, neither having done any good or evil, that the purpose of God according to election might stand, not of works, but of him that calleth (Rom. 9:11).

Even so then at this present time also there is a remnant according to the election of grace. And if by grace, then is it no more of works: otherwise grace is no more grace. But if it be of works, then it is no more grace: otherwise work is no more work (Rom. 11:5–6).

For by grace are ye saved through faith; and that not of yourselves: it is the gift of God: Not of works, lest any man should boast (Eph. 2:8–9).

Likewise, we must clearly understand there is not the slightest scriptural reference to an election of God whereby one person is chosen to be saved and another is not. In fact, John 3:15 tells us, *"That whosoever believeth in him should not perish, but have eternal life,"* and 2 Peter 3:9 states, *"The Lord is not slack concerning his promise, as some men count slackness; but is longsuffering to us-ward, not willing that any should perish, but that all should come to repentance."*

An individual is not saved because of God's choice alone. The individual must also choose to meet God's terms of salvation. God's plan is the same for all alike, and everyone, without exception, is invited, chosen, elected, foreknown, and predestined to salvation on the sole basis of the individual's choice and total conformity to the gospel. Otherwise, one will be lost, and there cannot be an exception to God's divine plan.

Ephesians 1:4 says that He has *"chosen us in him before the foundation of the world, that we should be holy and without blame before him in love."* Note God chose us before the foundation of the world—before sin even entered the world! God's choice is for all believers. The doctrine of God's choosing us for salvation is one of His greatest blessings because it guarantees our salvation. Realize also that God chose us not only for salvation but also for other reasons, such as:

- To bear not only fruit but lasting fruit (John 15:16)

- To be holy and blameless before Him in love (Eph. 1:4)

- To be a chosen generation, a royal priesthood, a holy nation, a peculiar people to show forth the praises of Him (Exod. 19:6; Deut. 7:6; 14:2; 1 Pet. 2:9)

- Fellow citizens with the saints and the household of God (Eph. 2:19)

- Salvation through sanctification of the Spirit and belief in the truth (2 Thess. 2:13)

Adopted Us

The second spiritual blessing in verse 5 is God *"adopted us,"* which means He predestinated us unto the adoption of children by Jesus Christ to Himself. God's unfolding plan for us not only includes salvation and personal transformation but also a warm, confident relationship with the Father. Verse 5 reveals Jesus Christ is an important part of this relationship and God's adoption plan. Not only did God choose us to be made holy, but He also grants us full status as His children, with all the benefits thereof.

As John 1:12 expresses, when we believe the gospel, we receive full access to God the Father, able to call out to Him as His children. Also, because we received the Spirit of adoption,[38] we have the privilege to cry, *"Abba, Father."*

> *But as many as received him, to them gave he power to become the sons of God, even to them that believe on his name* (John 1:12).

> *For ye have not received the spirit of bondage again to fear; but ye have received the Spirit of adoption, whereby we cry, Abba, Father. The Spirit itself beareth witness with our spirit, that we are the children of God* (Rom. 8:15–16).

[38] Dake, Finis, Jennings, *Dake's Annotated Reference Bible* (Ninth Printing edition), (Lawrenceville: Dake Publishing, Inc, 2006), 291, notes *q and *r.

Accepted Us

A sense of acceptance and belonging is one of our most basic human needs, and that is exactly what Jesus Christ gives us. God the Father accepts us, not based on who we are and what we have done, but on who Jesus Christ is and what He did.

This leads us to the third spiritual blessing in verse 6, where we are made "*accepted in the beloved.*" It is especially noteworthy to comprehend the beloved is Jesus Christ, as illustrated in Matthew 3:17; 17:5; Luke 3:22; and 2 Peter 21:17. When Jesus Christ was baptized, a voice from heaven said, "*This is my beloved Son, in whom I am well pleased*" (Matthew 3:17). So why didn't God just say, "accepted in Jesus Christ"? The answer is simple. God wants you to be conscious that you are now part of the family and beloved to Him the same way that Jesus Christ is.

Furthermore, the word *accepted* in the original Greek is a word far richer in meaning than the English translation can convey. It's the word *charitoo*,[39] which means "highly favored." This word is used only one other time in the Bible, when angel Gabriel appeared to Mary and said to her, "*Rejoice, highly favored [charitoo] one, the Lord is with you; blessed are you among women*" (Luke 1:28)!

---

[39] Strong's 5487: χαριτόω, charitoo (pronounced khar-ee-to'-o) from 5485; to grace, i.e., indue with special honor: —make accepted, be highly favored

Subsequently, we are not just accepted in the Beloved, which is already fantastic, but we are more precisely highly favored in the Beloved, Jesus Christ. When we put on Jesus Christ, the Father sees Jesus Christ's loveliness when He looks at us. The blood of Jesus Christ took away the guilt of our sins, and we stand before God the Father as perfectly accepted in the Beloved.

Redeemed Us

This leads us right into the fourth spiritual blessing recorded in verse 7, "*the redemption through His blood.*" As mentioned beforehand, to redeem means to buy back or secure the freedom of someone in bondage. Redemption is the price God paid to manifest His grace and adopt us as sons. Jesus Christ's blood stain should constantly remind everyone of His crucifixion and that His blood redeemed us and is essential in every part of life and service to Jesus Christ.

Redemption speaks of buying one's freedom and paying a ransom. The price for our sins, the payment to buy us out of eternal condemnation, was fully paid by the blood of Jesus Christ. In Jesus Christ, we are not any longer slaves to sin but become slaves to God. Since we are bought and paid for by His blood, we have an obligation to glorify God in our bodies and spirits.

> *For ye are bought with a price: therefore glorify*
> *God in your body, and in your spirit, which are*
> *God's* (1 Cor. 6:20).

Forgave Us

Verse 7 also describes the fifth spiritual blessing, *"the forgiveness of sins."* Forgiveness of sins is closely related to redemption but looks at the other side of the coin. When Jesus Christ paid the ransom for our sins, the debt of sin was canceled, and we were forgiven. Subsequently, we do not any longer have the burden of guilt and condemnation.

Sometimes after we confess our sins to God, we may not feel forgiven. But our feelings don't determine whether we're forgiven, our forgiveness is based on the blood of Jesus Christ. According to 1 John 1:9, if we confess our sins to God, we're forgiven and have the right to come boldly to Him. The separation is removed, and we can enjoy fellowship with Him once more.

> *There is therefore now no condemnation to*
> *them which are in Christ Jesus, who walk not*
> *after the flesh, but after the Spirit* (Rom. 8:1).

Revealed God's Will to Us

The sixth spiritual blessing is found in verses 9–10, *"Made know unto us the mystery of his will."* In other words, *revealed*

God's will to us, knowing the mystery of His will, centers on the fact that God has given us wisdom and insight through His Word and has shown us His desire to bring together in one all things in Jesus Christ[40] to glorify Him. Since all of creation was made by Him and is for His good pleasure, the consummation of His plan is when everything and everyone is brought in line to glorify Him.

> *Thou art worthy, O Lord, to receive glory and honour and power: for thou hast created all things, and for thy pleasure they are and were created* (Rev. 4:11).

By aligning ourselves with Him by faith, we become part of His perfect plan and purpose. God, without a doubt, is bringing everything together under the Lordship of Jesus Christ. He is setting apart for Himself the church as a redeemed bride. This is God's plan from beginning to end. While we do not completely experience this now when the times reach their fulfillment in the millennial reign of Jesus Christ, then everything will be subject to Him.[41] This is an amazing revelation! God, in Jesus Christ, is creating for Himself the church as a redeemed bride.

---

[40] Together in one all things in Jesus Christ refer to our position and one of the tenfold present state as Christians – Made both one in Christ. Jews and Gentiles make the New Testament Church (Ephesians 2:14-16; 3:6; 1 Corinthians 12:13)

[41] 1 Corinthians 15:24-29; Philippians 2:10-11; Revelation 21:1-4

And hath put all things under his feet, and gave
him to be the head over all things to the church,
Which is his body, the fulness of him that filleth
all in all (Eph. 1:22–23).

This is why God chose us, blessed us with all spiritual blessings, and lavished all wisdom and understanding on us— so we could understand His will and align ourselves with all that God has done since the beginning of time!

Inheritance Given to Us

We find the seventh spiritual blessing *"an inheritance"*[42] in verse 11. Also, we see three aspects of God's plan working together in verse 11. It begins with predestination, then shifts to His purpose, and then the counsel of His will.

In this verse, Apostle Paul assures the Ephesians and present-day believers of our inheritance (present and future) by reminding us that God predestined us to possess an inheritance. Just as God predestinated us unto the adoption of children by Jesus Christ to Himself, the second spiritual blessing mentioned above, God also predestined believers to receive an inheritance according to His purpose and counsel of His will.

The comfort to believers is that, while we were sinners and God's enemies (Rom. 5:8–10), God was delighted to choose a people for Himself. This was not a reckless and ill-conceived

---

[42] Strong's #2820: κληρόω, klēróō (pronounced klay-ro'-o) from G2819; to allot, i.e. (figuratively) to assign (a privilege):—obtain an inheritance

plan but was done according to God's purpose (cf. Eph. 3:11), counsel, and will. God called everyone, and all are free to accept or reject the call. For all who accept, God has fore-known and predestinated to be conformed to the image of his Son. In contrast, all who reject His plan, God has fore-known and predestinated them to spend eternal separation from Him.[43]

Apostle Peter, in 1 Peter 1:4, tells us four important qual-ities that distinguish our inheritance. First, our inheritance is *incorruptible*. What we have in Jesus Christ is not subject to corruption or decay. Second, our inheritance is *undefiled*. What we have in Jesus Christ is free from anything that would deform, debase, or degrade it. Third, our inheritance *does not fade away*. What we have in Jesus Christ is an enduring pos-session. Fourth, our inheritance is *reserved*. What we have in Jesus Christ is kept in heaven for us.

Sealed Us

The eighth spiritual blessing in verse 13 is that we are *"sealed with the Holy Spirit of promise."* The Holy Spirit's pres-ence in our lives acts as a seal, which indicates ownership and a guarantee of our inheritance. When Jesus Christ blood-stained us, He not only sheltered us under the blood stain, as sinners who fall short of the glory of God, but He also sealed

---

[43] Dake, Finis, Jennings, *Dake's Annotated Reference Bible* (Ninth Printing edition), (Lawrenceville: Dake Publishing, Inc, 2006), 292, note z.

us with the Holy Spirit of promise[44] to guide us into all truth and empower a righteous life.

Gave Us Down Payment of What's to Come; Guarantee Our Inheritance

The last of the nine spiritual blessings is in verse 14, *"Gave us down payment of what's to come; guarantee our inheritance."* When we become a child of God, He places His mark of ownership on us, guaranteeing our eternal security. As expressed in 2 Corinthians 5:5, God has given the earnest or the first-fruit of the Spirit as a guarantee that we will be resurrected and put on immortality. This is spoken of as the down payment of our full redemption, to hold us until the day Jesus Christ brings us to Him.

---

[44] *Chapter 8, I Am Drenched In the Blood of Jesus Christ, Blood Stained* further explains the concept of the sealing work of the Holy Spirit.

CHAPTER 8
I AM DRENCHED IN THE BLOOD OF JESUS CHRIST BLOOD STAINED

W e can only fully understand what drenched in the blood of Jesus Christ is by comprehending we are *Blood Bought, Blood Stained, and Blood Washed*. This chapter examines the second aspect: *Blood Stained*.

As Jesus Christ hung on the cross, His dripping blood stained everyone who acknowledged and confessed with their lips that Jesus Christ was Lord (recognizing His power, authority, and majesty as King of kings and Lord of lords) and in their hearts believed (adhere to, trust in and rely on the truth) God raised Him from the dead. Further, Jesus Christ's blood stain should constantly remind everyone of His crucifixion. His blood redeemed us and is essential in every part of life and service to Jesus Christ.

Paul stated in Galatians 2:20, *"I am crucified with Christ: nevertheless I live; yet not I, but*

Christ liveth in me: and the life which I now live in the flesh I live by the faith of the Son of God, who loved me, and gave himself for me" (Gal. 2:20).

Let's take a moment to examine Galatians 2:20 and how it applies to us being blood-stained by Jesus Christ. First of all, Jesus Christ brought man to the cross, so not only was Jesus Christ crucified at the cross but so was man. That is why we can proclaim, *"I am crucified with Christ: nevertheless I live: yet not I, but Christ lives in me."* He also bore our sins in His own body. We owed a great penalty for our own grievous sins, yet Jesus Christ paid the price for our sins.

Our sin was imputed to Jesus Christ, and His righteousness was imputed to us. Also, with Jesus Christ's crucifixion, we are crucified with Him. In His resurrection, we are raised with Him. Now we live an eternal life, though we are still on the earth in our mortal bodies. By faith, we need to remember we are in Jesus Christ, and having died with Him, we live with Him. All this ultimately caused us to be blood-stained! To be blood stained means we should die daily to our flesh,[45] live a life to serve Jesus Christ, and take up our cross to boldly follow Jesus Christ.

---

[45] Die daily to flesh – this refers to the outward man dying daily and not to dying to sin daily. Compare scriptures Psalm 44:22; Luke 9:23; Romans 8:36; 1 Corinthians15:31; 2 Corinthians 4:16; Ephesians 4:22-24

The song "Crucified with Christ," sung by Phillips, Craig, and Dean,[46] is a good rendition of the gratitude we should have for the crucifixion of Jesus Christ and the blood stain.

As I look back
On what I thought was living
I'm amazed at the price
I choose to pay
And to think I ignored
What really mattered
'Cause I thought the sacrifice
Would be too great
But when I finally reached
The point of giving in
I found the cross
Was calling even then
And even though
It took dying to survive
I've never felt so much alive
For I am crucified with Christ
And yet I live
Not I but Christ
That lives within me
His Cross will never ask for more

---

[46] "Crucified With Christ" Lyrics by Phillips, Craig and Dean from the album *Icon*. https://www.newreleasetoday.com/lyricsdetail.php?lyrics_id=98387. (Accessed June 26, 2021)

Than I can give
For it's not my strength but His
There's no greater sacrifice
For I am crucified with Christ

When Jesus Christ blood-stained us, He not only sheltered us under the blood stain, as sinners who fall short of the glory of God, but He also sealed us with the Holy Spirit of promise to guide us into all truth and empower a righteous life.

> *In whom ye also trusted, after that ye heard the word of truth, the gospel of your salvation: in whom also after that ye believed, ye were sealed with that holy Spirit of promise* (Eph. 1:13).

Sealed with the Holy Spirit

First and foremost, the seal is not a "what" but a "who"—the Holy Spirit! What does it mean to be sealed with the Holy Spirit? A seal is an identifying mark often placed on a letter, contract, or another document (Raymond, Erik. *What Does It Mean to Be Sealed with the Holy Spirit?*). The seal authenticates the contents. In the Old Testament, God set a sign on His chosen ones to mark or set them apart as His possession and protect and keep them from destruction (Ezek. 9:4–6).

In contrast, we see in Ephesians 1:13 that we are sealed with the Holy Spirit of promise. Then in John 6:27, we see God authenticating the relationship with His seal. Additionally, in Revelation 7:3, we read that God places a seal on His people to identify and protect them from wrath. All these Scriptures demonstrate that being sealed with the Holy Spirit communicates ownership, protection, security, and a validation of the relationship.

By giving us the Holy Spirit, the blood stain of Jesus Christ becomes prominent as the Holy Spirit continues to testify, authenticating the reality of our relationship by making us more and more like Jesus Christ.

We must, in the same way, come to the full realization that our Savior, Jesus Christ, also blood-stained us to carry the indelible mark of belonging to Him. Legally, God looks at the blood stain and sees us as if we had died with His Son, Jesus Christ. We see this in Galatians 6:17, where Paul speaks of bearing the marks of suffering for Jesus Christ. Likewise, we, too, must take a stand for the cross of Jesus Christ and accept the holy scars/marks that go with serving Jesus Christ as our Lord and Savior.

> *From henceforth let no man trouble me: for I*
> *bear in my body the marks[47] of the Lord Jesus*
> (Gal. 6:17).

---

[47] The Greek word for "marks" is stigma. Stigma (to "stick", i.e., prick): a mark incised or punched (for recognition of ownership), (fig.) scar of service:–mark.

We need to become conscious of the fact that the Holy Spirit is the Christian's seal. He seals us as God's people. In fact, Jesus Christ told us in John 16:7 that He had to go back to the Father for the Holy Spirit to come.

> *Nevertheless I tell you the truth; It is expedient for you that I go away: for if I go not away, the Comforter will not come unto you; but if I depart, I will send him unto you* (John 16:7).

Moreover, when Jesus Christ blood-stained us, it made it possible for the Holy Spirit to come to indwell or take up residence in all believers in Jesus Christ without exception. There are not any conditions placed upon this gift except faith in Jesus Christ. As such, the promised Holy Spirit guarantees and identifies God's people as His inheritance and we, as believers, belong to God as His children.

> *For ye have not received the spirit of bondage again to fear; but ye have received the Spirit of adoption, whereby we cry, Abba, Father. The Spirit itself beareth witness with our spirit, that we are the children of God* (Rom. 8:15–16).

> *Who hath also sealed us, and given the earnest of the Spirit in our hearts* (2 Cor. 1:22).

*And because ye are sons, God hath sent forth the
Spirit of his Son into your hearts, crying, Abba,
Father* (Gal. 4:6).

Indwell versus *Fill* with the Holy Spirit

Everyone must realize there is an important difference
between *indwell* and *fill* with the Holy Spirit. A quick study
of four Scriptures is essential to our understanding and ability
to distinguish *indwell* from *fill* with the Holy Spirit.

*And I will pray the Father, and he shall give
you another Comforter, that he may abide
with you for ever* (John 14:16).

*Jesus answered and said unto him, If a man
love me, he will keep my words: and my Father
will love him, and we will come unto him, and
make our abode with him* (John 14:23).

*But ye are not in the flesh, but in the Spirit, if
so be that the Spirit of God dwell in you. Now
if any man have not the Spirit of Christ, he is
none of his* (Rom. 8:9).

*And be not drunk with wine, wherein is excess;
but be filled with the Spirit* (Eph. 5:18).

After Jesus Christ ascended into heaven, He sent the promised Helper, the Holy Spirit. Jesus Christ promised the Holy Spirit would indwell believers and the indwelling would be permanent. The permanent indwelling of the Holy Spirit is not for a select few believers but for all believers. Let us examine three aspects of this concept.

First, the Holy Spirit is a gift given to all believers in Jesus Christ without exception, and there are not any conditions placed upon this gift except faith in Jesus Christ.

Second, the Holy Spirit is given at the moment of salvation. When we accept Jesus Christ, the Holy Spirit comes to abide/dwell/live in us.

> *In whom ye also trusted, after that ye heard the word of truth, the gospel of your salvation: in whom also after that ye believed, ye were sealed with that holy Spirit of promise* (Eph. 1:13).

Galatians 3:2 further emphasizes this same truth by connecting the Holy Spirit to the hearing of faith.

> *This only would I learn of you, Received ye the Spirit by the works of the law, or by the hearing of faith* (Gal. 3:2)?

Third, the Holy Spirit indwells believers permanently. The Holy Spirit is given to believers as a down payment or verification of their future glorification in Jesus Christ.

> *Who hath also sealed us, and given the earnest*
> *of the Spirit in our hearts* (2 Cor. 1:22).

> *And grieve not the holy Spirit of God, whereby*
> *ye are sealed unto the day of redemption*
> (Eph. 4:30).

Essentially, all believers in Jesus Christ have God's Holy Spirit living and dwelling within them.

Let us focus on *fill* with the Holy Spirit by examining Ephesians 5:18.

> *And be not drunk with wine, wherein is excess;*
> *but be filled with the Spirit* (Eph. 5:18).

This verse contrasts drunk with wine versus filled with the Holy Spirit. The central theme is one being controlled/influenced. The main idea Apostle Paul wants us to understand is one of being controlled by God's Spirit rather than by other forces. We can draw four conclusions from Ephesians 5:18.

1. Being drunk with wine in contrast to being filled with the Holy Spirit indicates being under control/influence. God wants us under the control/influence of and empowered by His Holy Spirit rather than by other forces.

2. We should be so completely yielded to the Holy Spirit that He can fully possess us, and in that sense, fill us—to be filled with the Holy Spirit is to be filled with Jesus Christ.

3. Being filled with the Holy Spirit implies freedom for the Holy Spirit to influence every part of our lives, guiding, instructing, teaching, controlling, and influencing us. Then His power will exert through us so what we do is fruitful to God, the Father.

4. We should be controlled/influenced by the Holy Spirit. And when controlled—not as a robot but as one who is influenced, led, and empowered by the Holy Spirit—the filling/replenishing by the Holy Spirit will cause the Lord Jesus Christ to walk around in our body and live His resurrected life in and through us.

In summary, from John 14:16, 23, Romans 8:9, and Ephesian 5:18, we learn three important concepts:

1. The Holy Spirit dwells (lives) in every believer forever,

2. The Holy Spirit comes on us to fill/replenish us and

3. The Holy Spirit indwells us at the time of our salvation, but we are filled/replenished with the Holy Spirit when we submit to the Holy Spirit.

Not Designed to "Run on Empty"

We must realize one reason we need the Holy Spirit to fill (replenish) us is that God did not design us to run on empty. He designed our spiritual gas tanks for the fullness of His Holy Spirit in our lives.

> *And to know the love of Christ, which passeth knowledge, that ye might be filled with all the fulness of God* (Eph. 3:19).

One purpose of the Holy Spirit is to fill us with the fullness of God and the overflowing presence of Jesus Christ. Therefore, when believers receive a fresh infilling of the Holy Spirit, we receive the fullness of God.

We should especially note to fill (replenish) with the Holy Spirit **is not a one-time event.** God designed us not only for His Spirit to indwell in us but for the Holy Spirit to constantly fill and replenish us until we begin to overflow as rivers of living water. The passages below illustrate this idea.

> *Thou preparest a table before me in the presence of mine enemies: thou anointest my head with oil; my cup runneth over* (Ps. 23:5).

> *He that believeth on me, as the scripture hath said, out of his belly shall flow rivers of living water. (But this spake he of the Spirit, which*

> *they that believe on him should receive: for*
> *the Holy Ghost was not yet given; because that*
> *Jesus was not yet glorified)* (John 7:38–39).

Likewise, the Bible makes it clear our lives should be one of continual fellowship with God, thus causing us to be continually filled with Him by His Holy Spirit. Again, the initial experience of being filled with the Holy Spirit **was never meant to be a one-time event.** Instead, we are meant to continually walk with the Lord and be ever-filled with His Holy Spirit.

Fill/Replenish with the Holy Spirit Is a Recurring Event!

We must always remember that to fill (replenish) with the Holy Spirit **is a recurring event.** We need continually filling/replenishing to renew (restore) our lives and ministries. It is our responsibility to be filled with the Holy Spirit.

How?

First, submit to the Holy Spirit and His instructing, teaching, guiding, controlling, influencing, leading, prompting, and unctioning. Second, reignite your passion with God. Never let the fire in your heart go out for God the Father.

The Bible makes it clear our lives should be one of continual fellowship with God, thus causing us to be continually filled with Him, with His Holy Spirit. As previously mentioned, this was never meant to be a one-time event.

111

Once we receive the Holy Spirit of God into our lives, the next step is to develop a lifestyle where the Holy Spirit continually fills us. We see this example from the apostles in their walk and lifestyle with God. For example, throughout the book of Acts, the apostles lived in such a way that the Holy Spirit continually filled them.

> *Then Peter, filled with the Holy Ghost, said unto them, Ye rulers of the people, and elders of Israel* (Acts 4:8).

> *Then Saul (who also is called Paul), filled with the Holy Ghost, set his eyes on him. And said, O full of all subtilty and all mischief, thou child of the devil, thou enemy of all righteousness, wilt thou not cease to pervert the right ways of the Lord* (Acts 13:9–10)?

> *And the disciples were filled with joy, and with the Holy Ghost* (Acts 13:52).

Of particular note is the account of Stephen's speech recorded in Acts 7. Stephen, under the anointing of the Holy Spirit, brought an indictment against his accusers for resisting the Holy Spirit (Acts 7:1–53). After Stephen shared his faith in Jesus Christ, the rebellious religious leaders stoned him to death. However, even at the time of his death, Stephen was so filled with the Holy Spirit that he *"gazed into heaven, saw the heavens opened and the glory of God and Jesus Christ standing at the right hand of God"* (Acts 7:55–56).

Carry the Blood-Stained Banner

As born-again believers, we must bear the marks and carry the blood-stained banner[48] of the cross. To do this, we first need to comprehend the meaning of Jehovah-Nissi as expressed in Exodus 17:15. Jehovah-Nissi is God's name, which means "The Lord Our Banner."[49] The Lord is our banner in that He is the One under whom we unite. He is our Savior.

We are rescued by Him and identified in Him. Moreover, the Lord is our banner because we live to celebrate and honor His faithfulness to us. The Lord is our banner because He identifies us as children of God. The Lord is our banner because of the saving work of Jesus Christ. The Lord is our banner because we represent Him to the world.

In case you did not catch it, there is also a hidden anticipation of Jesus Christ in Jehovah-Nissi. Isaiah 11:10 predicts the coming of Jesus Christ, who will stand as a banner for the people.

---

[48] A banner is something that identifies and unifies a particular group of people. https://www.gotquestions.org/Lord-is-my-banner.html

[49] Dake, Finis, Jennings, *Dake's Annotated Reference Bible* (Ninth Printing edition), (Lawrenceville: Dake Publishing, Inc, 2006), 77, 16 Jehovah Titles.

> *And in that day there shall be a root of Jesse,*
> *which shall stand for an ensign of the people;*
> *to it shall the Gentiles seek: and his rest shall*
> *be glorious* (Isa. 11:10).

The ensign refers to a standard or a banner around which the nations shall rally. The Messiah Himself will be the rallying point for all nations. To Him, they will come, and in Him, they will put their trust.

> *And he shall set up an ensign for the nations,*
> *and shall assemble the outcasts of Israel, and*
> *gather together the dispersed of Judah from the*
> *four corners of the earth* (Isa. 11:12).

Psalm 60:4 and Isaiah 13:2 further mention that we are given a banner to display because of the truth and to exalt Jesus Christ before the world. In other words, when we lift up the blood-stained banner, we actually lift up Jesus Christ as our banner. We proclaim we belong to Him, identify ourselves by His name, and find comfort in His salvation, security, and victory. We need to lift up the blood-stained banner and boldly preach the gospel of Jesus Christ to draw people to Him.

> *Thou hast given a banner to them that fear thee,*
> *that it may be displayed because of the truth.*
> *Selah* (Ps. 60:4).

> *Lift ye up a banner upon the high mountain,*
> *exalt the voice unto them, shake the hand,*
> *that they may go into the gates of the nobles*
> (Isa. 13:2).

> *And I, if I be lifted up from the earth, will draw*
> *all men unto me* (John 12:32).

Become conscious of the fact that Satan, demons, and the host of demonic forces want us to be unaware we are blood-stained and given a blood-stained banner to lift up. Why? The blood stain hides us, and as long as we stay hidden by Jesus Christ's blood stain, we eventually begin to smell like God, talk and think like God and become the image of Jesus Christ.

When this phenomenon occurs, and Satan sees you serving a purpose and fulfilling destiny on earth, he and his demons do not see you but the blood-stained banner of Jesus Christ, His blood profusely permeating over, concealing, and protecting you! Additionally, Satan wants us to be ignorant of the fact that when we lift up Jesus Christ, all men will be drawn to Jesus Christ and freed from Satan's lies.

CHAPTER 9
I AM DRENCHED IN THE BLOOD OF JESUS CHRIST BLOOD WASHED

᷂

W e can only fully understand what drenched in the blood of Jesus Christ is by comprehending we are *Blood Bought, Blood Stained, and Blood Washed.* This chapter examines the third aspect: *Blood Washed.*

As the old hymn says, *"What can wash away my sin? Nothing but the blood of Jesus; What can make me whole again? Nothing but the blood of Jesus. Oh! precious is the flow That makes me white as snow; No other fount I know, Nothing but the blood of Jesus."*[50]

Being blood washed by the blood of Jesus Christ helps us experience the fullness of the kingdom of God and His righteousness. Also, Psalm 24:3–4 tells us that being blood washed is needed to clean our hands and purify our hearts.

---

[50] What Can Wash Away My Sin Lyrics. https://www.lyricsondemand. com/miscellaneouslyrics/christianlyrics/whatcanwashawaymysinlyrics. html

This washing by the blood of Jesus Christ makes it possible for us to ascend into the hill of the Lord as well as stand in His holy place.

The Heart Is Deceitful Above All Things and Desperately Wicked

Jeremiah 4:14 compares the cleansing of our souls and hearts from evil sin and wickedness to a washing!

> *O Jerusalem, wash thine heart from wickedness, that thou mayest be saved. How long shall thy vain thoughts lodge within thee* (Jer. 4:14)?

Additionally, Jeremiah 17:9 lets us know every person's heart is deceitful above all things and desperately wicked. Since this wickedness can defile us and our nature, we stand in need of blood washing. The blood of Jesus Christ functions to convince us of the wickedness and pollution of our hearts. However, we are incapable of washing ourselves from this wickedness. Only God Himself is capable of searching the heart to blood wash it from this wickedness. It is the precious blood of Jesus Christ, by which only the heart is thoroughly washed and purified, that inevitably cause us to have clean hands and create in us purified hearts.

Furthermore, to be supernaturally changed is the only hope for the wicked and sinful human heart. Thankfully, God, in the passage below, gives the solution. Where sin was once inscribed on the hearts of His people, God provides a new inscription:

> *But this shall be the covenant that I will make*
> *with the house of Israel; After those days, saith*
> *the Lord, I will put my law in their inward*
> *parts, and write it in their hearts; and will*
> *be their God, and they shall be my people*
> (Jer. 31:33).

The Blood Of Jesus Christ Continually Washes Us:
Washing of Water by the Word of God

Remember, at the cross, our Lord Jesus Christ not only became sin for us, but He also took the blame and bore the wrath so we stand forgiven at the cross. But it was also at the cross where Jesus Christ used His servant body to carry our sins to the cross and His physical act of bleeding on the cross (followed by His death and resurrection) washed away our human sins and continually washes us from all sin, so we can live free the right way in righteousness.

> *For he hath made him to be sin for us, who*
> *knew no sin; that we might be made the righ-*
> *teousness of God in him* (2 Cor. 5:21).

> *Who his own self bare our sins in his own body*
> *on the tree, that we, being dead to sins, should*

live unto righteousness: by whose stripes ye were healed (1 Pet. 2:24).

Not only does the blood of Jesus Christ continually wash us from all sin, but as noted in John 15:3, *"Now ye are clean through the word which I have spoken unto you,"* the Word of God also washes us. Recall, if you will, Apostle John states, in John 1:1, *"the Word was with God and the Word was God."* In other words, John presents Jesus Christ as the pre-incarnate God of creation and the Word of God or expression of God, as well as the Savior of the world. Jesus Christ is the Word of God made flesh, dwelt among us, and everyone who believes in Him is washed, sanctified, and cleansed by the washing of water by the Word of God.

To further increase our understanding, let's focus on what Apostle Paul wrote in Ephesians 5:26–27. These verses describe the process Jesus Christ uses to perfect the church (body of believers) to present it as holy and without blemish.

> *That he might sanctify and cleanse it with the washing of water by the word, That he might present it to himself a glorious church, not having spot, or wrinkle, or any such thing; but that it should be holy and without blemish* (Eph. 5:26–27).

Subsequently, we need to clearly understand that the washing of water by the Word of God is more than a simple washing of water. Jesus Christ undoubtedly understood His purpose to die for the sins of mankind and His blood of the (new and better) covenant, which (ratifies the agreement and) was to be poured out for many (as a substitutionary atonement for the forgiveness of sins).

Furthermore, the washing of water by the Word of God is not just of contact with the blood of Jesus Christ but of total immersion in this atoning of Jesus Christ's blood that washed us, serves as the source of our redemption, and provides a stronger washing and means of forgiveness than mere water alone. Essentially, the washing of water by the Word of God washes us deep down inside our very souls. It washes us thoroughly of our iniquity and cleanses us from our sins. Additionally, it purifies our thoughts, scrubs our motives, and washes our conscience as we absorb the Word of God and obey its truths.

Wash Me Thoroughly from My Iniquity and Cleanse Me from My Sin

King David wrote Psalm 51 during his blackest hour of self-awareness after committing adultery with Bathsheba and murdering her husband, Uriah. This psalm records David's sincere repentance and confession. David, believing God abounds in mercy, requests forgiveness and washing and makes an earnest plea before God:

> *Wash me throughly from mine iniquity, and cleanse me from my sin* (Ps. 51:2).

> *Purge me with hyssop, and I shall be clean: wash me, and I shall be whiter than snow* (Ps. 51:7).

> *Create in me a clean heart, O God; and renew a right spirit within me* (Ps. 51:10).

Let us take a moment to first examine hyssop, a small shrub used in the ceremonial cleansing of people and houses. For instance, in Exodus 12:13, 22, we see the Israelites applied animals' blood to their doorposts as protection against the plague. God promised that disaster would not touch the Israelites when He smote the land of Egypt, and He would pass over the Israelites when He saw the blood.

> *And the blood shall be to you for a token upon the houses where ye are: and when I see the blood, I will pass over you, and the plague shall not be upon you to destroy you, when I smite the land of Egypt* (Exod. 12:13).

> *And ye shall take a bunch of hyssop, and dip it in the blood that is in the bason, and strike the lintel and the two side posts with the blood that is in the bason; and none of you shall go*

out at the door of his house until the morning
(Exod. 12:22).

In Leviticus 14:6–7, we witness the priest dipped hyssop in the sacrificial blood of an animal and sprinkled it seven times on the person needing cleansing from leprosy.

> *As for the living bird, he shall take it, and the cedar wood, and the scarlet, and the hyssop, and shall dip them and the living bird in the blood of the bird that was killed over the running water: And he shall sprinkle upon him that is to be cleansed from the leprosy seven times, and shall pronounce him clean, and shall let the living bird loose into the open field*
> (Lev. 14:6–7).

In Psalm 51:7, David symbolically referred to hyssop to tell God about his longing for purification from his sin. David, a man after God's own heart, knew he had sinned against God and done evil in His sight. David also understood God could forgive and wash him clean of his sin to make him whiter than snow. *Whiter than snow* figuratively expresses the condition of one who has received God's forgiveness, cleansing from sin, and redemption. We must understand David does not refer to physical cleansing. Rather, he asked God to wash him spiritually as he confessed his sin.

David's earnest plea before God foreshadows Isaiah:

Wash you, make you clean; put away the evil of your doings from before mine eyes; cease to do evil (Isa. 1:16).

Come now, and let us reason together, saith the Lord: though your sins be as scarlet, they shall be as white as snow; though they be red like crimson, they shall be as wool (Isa. 1:18).

Ultimately, God washes away the stains of our sinful past so we are absolutely made white as snow and wool, which is not dyed white but naturally white. Our God washes the traces of sin from us so deeply that we are as clean and white as if we had never sinned! God's washing by the blood of Jesus Christ is utterly effective.

Subsequently, we should learn from David, the sinner who sees his need and gives himself to God, that God will be just in washing (cleansing) the sinner from all sins and making him His son and joint-heir with Jesus Christ. Furthermore, David's earnest plea to be washed and made whiter than snow prefigured ***the greater, more perfect*** appropriation of God's grace, forgiveness, and salvation made available through the sacrifice of the blood of the Lamb, our Lord Jesus Christ.

Just like King David, we all have sinned and come short of the glory of God. Therefore, we must repent and draw near to the Lord Jesus Christ in our blackest moments of failure. In these moments of failure, we must ask Jesus Christ, who loves, washes, and frees us from our sins in his blood, to forgive and wash our guilt-stained souls whiter than snow.

> *And from Jesus Christ, who is the faithful wit-ness, and the first begotten of the dead, and the prince of the kings of the earth. Unto him that loved us, and washed us from our sins in his own blood* (Rev. 1:5).

In comparison, Revelation 7:14 represents the act of faith whereby the believing sinner trusts in the Lord Jesus Christ, who, by His blood, is blood-washed and makes the believer clean and white in the sight of God.

> *And I said unto him, Sir, thou knowest. And he said to me, These are they which came out of great tribulation, and have washed their robes, and made them white in the blood of the Lamb* (Rev. 7:14).

This verse describes a group of redeemed people as those who washed their robes and made them white in the blood of the Lamb. We must never forget there is nothing we can do to wash ourselves of sin. But it is only through Jesus Christ's sacrifice on the cross—the shedding of His precious blood—that we are blood washed, redeemed, and rescued from the kingdom of darkness and transferred to the kingdom of God (Col. 1:13, 20; Eph. 1:7).

Walk in the Light, as He Is in the Light

We can be forgiven and washed of every sin by the blood of Jesus Christ. In essence, this washing removes the punishment of sin and separation between God and us.

> *But if we walk in the light, as he is in the light, we have fellowship one with another, and the blood of Jesus Christ his Son cleanseth us from all sin* (1 John 1:7).

> *If we confess our sins, he is faithful and just to forgive us our sins, and to cleanse us from all unrighteousness* (1 John 1:9).

Let us take a moment now to examine 1 John 1:7, 9. It is the blood of Jesus Christ that washes us from all sin from the time of confession of sin and as long as we walk in the light. Further, it is the blood that makes us a new creature in Jesus Christ. Also, it is the blood that washes and sets us free from our past, causing old things to pass away and all things become new (2 Corinthians 5:17).

As stated in 1 John 1:7, walking in the light, having fellowship with one another, and being blood washed (cleansed) from sin are vital provisions of the blood of Jesus Christ. If we walk in the light, then the first result is fellowship with one another, and the second result is that the blood of the Lamb blood-washed us from all sin.

All three verbs—walking, having fellowship, being washed—are in the continuous present tense. They do not just happen once, they must go on continually. We must continually walk in the light to continue having fellowship with one another and for the blood of Jesus Christ to continually wash us.

Even though we may claim to be blood washed by the blood of Jesus Christ, when we do not meet the provisions of 1 John 1:7, we are not truly washed. Realize the blood of Jesus Christ does not wash us in the dark but only as we walk in the light.

The first test of whether we walk in the light is whether we fellowship with one another. Unfortunately, when we do not enjoy fellowship with our fellow believers and, most importantly, with the Lord Jesus Christ, then we are not in the light.

His blood now speaks for us and washes us from all sin! As we see in 1 John 1:9, God not only forgives our past sins but for anything we do now, we can appropriate the blood of Jesus Christ. When we repent, we come into agreement with what the blood speaks. Realize repentance is essential to agree with the blood of Jesus Christ! Repentance brings things to the light, allowing us to come out of darkness, choose light over darkness, see the difference between Satan and God, and choose God over Satan.

> *If we confess our sins, he is faithful and just to forgive us our sins, and to cleanse us from all unrighteousness* (1 John 1:9).

It is the blood that cleanses us from all sin from the time of the confession of sin and as long as we walk in the light. It is the blood that makes us a new creature in Jesus Christ and sets us free from our past, causing old things to pass away and all things become new.

> *To open their eyes, and to turn them from darkness to light, and from the power of Satan unto God, that they may receive forgiveness of sins, and inheritance among them which are sanctified by faith that is in me* (Acts 26:18).

As mentioned before, when we stumble, we are called to confess our sins and come to a place where we willingly acknowledge our wrongdoing and ask God for forgiveness. Once we do this, God will forgive us! We are cleansed from all sin from the time of the confession of sin and as long as we walk in the light!

It is especially noteworthy to understand if we claim we experience a shared life with Jesus Christ and continue to stumble around in the dark, we are obviously lying and do not know the truth – we are not living what we claim.

Additionally, as previously mentioned, if we claim that we have never sinned, we out-and-out contradict God—make a liar out of Him.

Walking in the light means we consider Jesus Christ as the light of this world, and we walk in this light by following His precepts, living in His awesome power, and growing in His grace. Walking in the light directly relates to following Jesus Christ, who said, *"I am the light of the world. He who follows me shall not walk in darkness, but have the light of life. As long as I am in the world, I am the light of the world"* (John 8:12; 9:5).

Walking in the light is a continuous process related to spiritual growth and taking steps toward maturity. It is growing in holiness and maturing in faith as we follow Jesus Christ, the light of the world and the opposite of evil. Furthermore, our God calls us to live in the light He graciously gives us and walk as children of light.

> *For ye were sometimes darkness, but now are ye light in the Lord: walk as children of light* (Eph. 5:8).

Here's another way to put it, God calls us the light of the world. As a city set on a hill cannot be hidden, so it is with us as children of light and the light of the world. Our light needs to shine before men that they may see our good works and glorify our Father, who is in heaven (Matt. 5:14–16).

Equally important to consider is that sin begins its reign in our minds, which is why it is always crucial to examine what we think. Realize it is not the passing lustful thought that is sinful but rather when we dwell on it, imagining what it would be like. As long as we reject those thoughts, we will do what God called us to do and walk in the light and freedom of His truth.

We should use our powerful God tools to smash these warped philosophies, tearing down barriers erected against the truth of God, fitting every loose thought, emotion, and impulse into the structure of life that is shaped by Jesus Christ, and bring them into captivity to the obedience of Jesus Christ. Our tools are ready at hand for clearing the ground of every obstruction and building lives of obedience into maturity.

> *(For the weapons of our warfare are not carnal, but mighty through God to the pulling down of strong holds;) Casting down imaginations, and every high thing that exalteth itself against the knowledge of God, and bringing into captivity every thought to the obedience of Christ* (2 Cor. 10:4–5).

The Washing of Regeneration

Regeneration refers to the new birth, second birth, or being born again to see the kingdom of God! In His conversation with Nicodemus, Jesus Christ stated three times the necessity of the new birth or to be born again. This new birth or to be born again, which Jesus Christ mentioned to Nicodemus is a spiritual, holy, and heavenly birth, that make us spiritually alive as a result of faith in Jesus Christ.

> *Jesus answered and said unto him, Verily, verily, I say unto thee, Except a man be born again, he cannot see the kingdom of God* (John 3:3).
> *Jesus answered, Verily, verily, I say unto thee, Except a man be born of water and of the Spirit, he cannot enter into the kingdom of God* (John 3:5).
> *Marvel not that I said unto thee, Ye must be born again* (John 3:7).

As these Scriptures attest, without the washing of regeneration, there is no seeing nor entering the kingdom of God. Unless we are blood washed by the blood of Jesus Christ and the washing of water by the Word of God, we cannot have any part nor portion with Jesus Christ in the heavenly glory.

Regeneration radically changes us. In our natural state, we are "dead in trespasses and sins (Eph. 2:1)" until Jesus Christ makes us spiritually alive. Just as our physical birth fits us for the earth, our spiritual rebirth fits us for heaven to sit together in Christ Jesus.

> *And hath raised us up together, and made us*
> *sit together in heavenly places in Christ Jesus*
> (Eph. 2:6).

The washing of regeneration makes us spiritually astute to see, hear, seek after divine things, and live a life of faith and holiness. Additionally, as regeneration has a way of causing Jesus Christ to develop deep in our hearts, we partake of the divine nature and are made new creatures. It is due to the washing of regeneration that we look inside, and what we see is anyone united with the Messiah gets a fresh start, and is created new. The old life is gone, a new life in Jesus Christ emerges!

> *Therefore if any man be in Christ, he is a new*
> *creature: old things are passed away; behold,*
> *all things are become new* (2 Cor. 5:17).

We need to clearly understand that the source of this transformation is God, not man. God's great love and free gift, His rich grace, and abundant mercy, cause our rebirth. The mighty power of God—the same mighty power that raised Jesus Christ from the dead—is displayed in the regeneration and conversion of sinners (Eph. 1:19–20).

The washing of regeneration is necessary. Sinful human flesh cannot stand in God's holy presence. Realize regeneration is not optional, for *"flesh gives birth to flesh, but the Spirit gives birth to spirit"* (John 3:6). Likewise, regeneration is part of what God does for us at the moment of salvation, seals us with the Holy Spirit of promise (Eph. 1:13), adopts us as children by Jesus Christ to Himself (Eph. 1:5; Gal. 4:5), and redeems us through Jesus Christ's blood (Eph. 1:7).

The Washing of Regeneration and Renewing of the Holy Spirit

Not by works of righteousness which we have done, but according to his mercy he saved us, by the washing of regeneration, and renewing of the Holy Ghost; Which he shed on us abundantly through Jesus Christ our Saviour (Titus 3:5–6).

Titus 3:5–6 is not an illusion to the incidental physical washing the water of baptism might do but refers to the washing away of our sins (via the precious blood of Jesus Christ) that occurs when we are born again. At the moment of new birth or to be born again, we are made a new creature in Jesus Christ, and old things are passed away, behold, all things become new (2 Cor. 5:17). In other words, at our new birth, our Lord Jesus Christ stepped in to save us from our sinful nature.

Take note, Jesus Christ blood-washed us. He gave us a good washing, and we came out a new people, washed inside through and through by the renewing of the Holy Spirit. Our Savior Jesus Christ poured out a new life, a new birth so generously. God's gift restored our relationship with Him and gave us back our lives. And there's more life to come—an eternity of life! You can count on this. Furthermore, the Lord regenerates us by renewing our minds so we can walk in the center of His will, plan, purpose, and destiny.

Titus 3:5–6 brings together the Holy Spirit's eternal impacts on our lives (regeneration and renewing) in a rather unique way. To begin, God saved us through the washing of regeneration and the renewing of the Holy Spirit. Second, regeneration and renewing come together only in this passage. Third, as previously mentioned, regeneration refers to the new birth, second birth, or being born again whereas renewing (anakaínōsis is the Greek for renewing[51]) refers to being made new again and different as the supernatural work of the Holy Spirit. Renewing by the Holy Spirit, in terms of Titus 3:5, serves to connect us to the washing of regeneration and salvation. In other words, salvation renewal by the Holy Spirit brings the believer into a new and different life in Jesus Christ.

The following statement best expresses the focus of Titus 3:5: the washing of regeneration purges away the old things of our natural life, and the renewing of the Holy Spirit reconstitutes and transforms us with the divine life and divine nature into the image of God. Therefore, let's take a moment to explore these elements of the renewing of the Holy Spirit—divine life and divine nature.

---

[51] Strong's #342 anakaínōsis (from 303 /aná, "up, completing a process," which intensifies kainō, "make fresh, new"; see 2537 /kainós) – properly, a new development; a renewal, achieved by God's power.

The Divine Life

The divine life God calls us to live is to walk in the Spirit with the realization Jesus Christ died in the flesh. However, God calls us not to die in the flesh like His Son, Jesus Christ, did but to die daily in the flesh because Jesus Christ must increase, but we must decrease!

What does this mean for our lives? All of us must decrease (be done away with) so the life of Jesus Christ can increase (form) in us. Every single reference and focus to myself must surrender to the Lord Jesus Christ. Our outward man perishes, yet the inward man is daily renewed in the image of Jesus Christ. We must decrease, and Jesus Christ must increase until we are nothing and He is everything!

The new divine life Jesus Christ gives us His own perfect life, it is His glorious life living through us. He came so we could have Him, the divine life. It is Jesus Christ's risen life working in us that becomes our lives.

Living the divine life Jesus Christ's way is a continuous, progressive walk with the Lord, which can become increasingly difficult. The divine life is death to self, but it produces the life of Jesus Christ in us. In due time, the divine life we live is to be an expression of Jesus Christ and not ourselves.

Galatians 2:20 illustrates the divine life God calls us to live:

I am crucified with Christ: nevertheless I live;
yet not I, but Christ liveth in me: and the life
which I now live in the flesh I live by the faith of

> *the Son of God, who loved me, and gave him-*
> *self for me* (Gal. 2:20).

This verse tells us Jesus Christ was crucified for our sins and we are crucified with Jesus Christ and live with Him. By faith, we trust that His death paid for our own sins. In this way, we and our sins are crucified with Him on the cross. That sinful "us" dies, replaced by the resurrected Jesus Christ "in us." Even though we continue to live in the flesh, of course, our lives are now directed not by our sinful selves but by our faith in our Lord Jesus Christ. Therefore, it is really not our lives. But it is the life of Jesus Christ that we partake of and now live in the flesh by the faith of the Son of God, who loved us and made it possible for us to live by faith. This is the epitome of divine life!

The renewing of the Holy Spirit helps us to come to the point of not responding to our soul/flesh desires, those desires that are pleasing in our own eyesight, and live a life pleasing to God and not a self-absorbed life but instead a God-absorbed life.

> *So then they that are in the flesh cannot please*
> *God. But ye are not in the flesh, but in the Spirit,*
> *if so be that the Spirit of God dwell in you. Now*
> *if any man have not the Spirit of Christ, he is*
> *none of his. And if Christ be in you, the body is*
> *dead because of sin; but the Spirit is life because*
> *of righteousness. But if the Spirit of him that*

> *raised up Jesus from the dead dwell in you, he*
> *that raised up Christ from the dead shall also*
> *quicken your mortal bodies by his Spirit that*
> *dwelleth in you* (Rom. 8:8–11).

As evident in Romans 8:8–11, Christians do not mind the things of the flesh but of the Spirit when the Spirit dwells in them. When we do not have the Spirit, then we do not belong to Jesus Christ.

When Jesus Christ is in you, the body is dead to all sin, and the Spirit dominates your life as you live to all righteousness. When this happens, we can expect a quickening for our mortal bodies by the Spirit that dwells in us. In essence, those who trust God's action in them find that God's Spirit is in them—living and breathing God!

The Divine Nature

The Holy Spirit renews us not only with the divine life but also with the divine nature. In 2 Peter 1:3–4, we witness the renewing of the Holy Spirit makes believers "partakers of the divine nature" through God's promises, but what does that mean, exactly? To what extent can we, as believers, partake of God's nature?

> *According as his divine power hath given unto*
> *us all things that pertain unto life and godliness,*
> *through the knowledge of him that hath called*

> *us to glory and virtue: Whereby are given unto*
> *us exceeding great and precious promises: that*
> *by these ye might be partakers of the divine*
> *nature, having escaped the corruption that is*
> *in the world through lust* (2 Pet. 1:3–4).

There are several notable points in 2 Peter 1:3–4. First, God's power grants us the ***very great promises*** concerning our salvation. Second, it is through these promises we are made ***partakers of the divine nature.*** Third, as partakers of the divine nature, we escape the world's decay and rise above sinful desires. Simply put, when we are saved, we receive a new nature, by which we do not perish with the world.

Human nature in the Bible is what makes us "us." A person's nature is the sum total of qualities that make the person who the person is. It is a person's inherent character, which constitutes individuality.[52] Romans 5:12; 7:14 informs us every human being is born with Adam's nature, which is sinful and causes us to naturally bend toward pleasing self—doing those things that are right in our own eyesight and not God's. However, our natural selves cannot please God.[53] Our sinful nature prevents fellowship and intimacy with God, retains us in bondage to sin, and eventually leads to spiritual death.[54] In

---

[52] https://coggle.it/diagram/W795CRyZUbBIXibA/t/personality-reacting-to-other-people

[53] Romans 8:8

[54] Romans 6:16, 23; 7:14; 2 Peter 2:19

essence, we cannot free ourselves from sin because we cannot change our nature, only the washing of regeneration and renewing of the Holy Spirit can do that.

When we are baptized with the Holy Spirit, we are renewed to the pre-fall condition of being indwelt by the Holy Spirit. We are restored to spiritual fellowship with God as if we were sinless like Adam and Eve before they disobeyed God and ate the fruit of the tree that was in the midst of the garden. Receiving God's Holy Spirit brings us to life spiritually and gives us eternal life.

We are regenerated (born again spiritually) by the renewing of the Holy Spirit. The fifteen factors below outline the renewing work of the Holy Spirit.

1. True worship of God (John 4:24; Phil. 3:3)
2. Spiritual fellowship (2 Cor. 13:14)
3. Transforms into the image of Christ (2 Cor. 3:18; Gal. 4:19)
4. Intercessor of prayer (Rom. 8:26–27; Jude 20)
5. Glorifies Jesus Christ (John 16:14–15)
6. Teaches and recalls the Word of God (John 14:26; 16:12–15; 1 John 2:27)
7. Bears witness of Jesus Christ (John 15:26)
8. Guides and discloses all divine truth (John 8:32; 16:13)
9. Reveals the thoughts of God (1 Cor. 2:9-13)
10. Ability to use the Word of God as a spiritual weapon in angelic conflict (Eph. 6:17)
11. Pours the love of God within the heart (Rom. 5:5)

12. Bears witness with our spirit that we are children of God (Rom. 8:15–17)
13. Spirituality (1 Cor. 2:15; 3:1)
14. Spiritually gifted ministry in church (1 Cor. 12:1–11; Heb. 2:4)
15. Restrainer of old sin-nature (Gal. 5:16–17; Rom. 8:1–4)

When we believe in the Lord Jesus Christ, confess with our mouth the Lord Jesus Christ, and believe in our hearts that God raised Jesus Christ from the dead, we are saved.[55] At that moment, we undergo a radical spiritual transformation. This is what the Apostle Peter means when he says we are made partakers of the divine nature. We are made new creatures in Jesus Christ; we are born again. We died, and now our lives are "hidden with Jesus Christ in God."[56] We are "in Christ Jesus" and walk not after the flesh but after the Spirit.[57]

God is faithful to keep His "great and precious promises" and we should praise Him for our Savior and Redeemer, Jesus Christ, the gift of the Holy Spirit, and the everlasting life we enjoy as partakers of His divine nature. As partakers of the divine nature:

1. Believers do not have to follow their sinful nature any longer.

---

[55] Acts 16:31; Romans 10:9

[56] Colossians 3:3

[57] Romans 8:1

2. At salvation, our old nature is passed away; all things become new—we receive a new divine nature that desires the things of God (2 Cor. 5:17).

3. Our old way of life was nailed to the cross with Jesus Christ, a decisive end to that sin-miserable life. We are not any longer enslaved to the passions and sins of the flesh (Rom. 6:6, 14).

4. We have a faithful God who will never let us be pushed past our limit but will also make a way to escape the temptation so that we may be able to bear it (1 Cor. 10:13).

5. God gives us His nature, makes us His sons and daughters, and conforms us to the image of His Son (Rom. 8:29; 2 Cor. 6:18).

6. The Holy Spirit indwells in us. God declares we are "more than conquerors" because of the power, might, and strength of the Holy Spirit within our hearts (Rom. 8:37).

7. Our Comforter, the Holy Spirit, will abide with us forever. We will never be forsaken (John 14:16; Heb. 13:5).

Ten Facts about the New Birth

Understand the only means of regeneration is by faith in the finished work of Jesus Christ on the cross. Regardless of the amount of good works we do or how well we keep the law, it can regenerate our hearts and cause the new birth to happen. We do not need renovation or reformation or reorganization, we need the washing of regeneration, and we need the new birth. Let's take a moment to look at ten facts about the new birth.[58]

1. A moral and spiritual change, not a physical one (John 3:1–8; Gal. 4:29)
2. A change of heart, will, motives, desires, life, and conduct (2 Cor. 5:17–18)
3. A change of masters, not constitutional makeup of body, soul, or spirit (Rom. 6:11–23; 8:1–4)
4. Adoption of one from the satanic family into the family of God (Rom. 8:14–16; Gal. 4:5; Eph. 1:5)
5. Not a coming into existence of the body, soul, or spirit, as in the natural birth, but a consecration of them to serve God and holiness instead of Satan and sin (Rom. 6:16–22; 8:1–13; Gal. 5:16–26; Col. 3:5–10)
6. Not a begetting by the Holy Spirit in the sense that Jesus Christ became and is the only begotten Son of God (John 1:14, 18; 3:16) but renewal in righteousness and true holiness of one who is already in existence (Ps. 51:10; Eph. 4:23–24; Col. 3:10)
7. A change of nature, but not the coming into existence of that nature (Rom. 3:24–25; 2 Cor. 5:17; Titus 3:5)
8. A change of favor, a new standing before God (Rom. 5:1–2; Eph. 2:1–9; Titus 2:11–14; 2 Pet. 3:18; 1 John 3:8–10)

---

[58] Dake, Finis, Jennings, *Dake's Annotated Reference Bible* (Ninth Printing edition), (Lawrenceville: Dake Publishing, Inc, 2006), 358, note d.

9. A change of character, state, and service (Rom. 3:24–31; 5:1–11; 1 Cor. 13; Gal. 5:21–22; 2 Tim. 2:21; Titus 2:11–14)

10. There is not any comparison between natural and spiritual birth as to choose in the matter, conception, embryo, process, and actual birth. The very moment one is grown enough to recognize he is a sinner, repents, and believes the gospel, a moral and spiritual change takes place (Mark 1:15; Rom. 1:16; 10:9–10; 2 Cor. 5:17–18; Eph. 2:8–9; 1 John 1:9)

CHAPTER 10
I AM DRENCHED IN THE BLOOD OF JESUS CHRIST PLEAD THE BLOOD OF JESUS CHRIST

O ur fundamental understanding concludes with pleading[59] the blood of Jesus Christ. In the early days of the Pentecostal outpouring, some of the old-timers used to frequently say, "*I plead the blood! I plead the blood of Jesus Christ!*" We, as born-again believers, must restore this powerful phrase to our vocabulary because there is still much power in the blood of Jesus Christ!

We oftentimes sing songs about pleading the blood. These songs stir our emotions and excite our flesh but do very little to help the listener understand the spiritual significance of what

---

[59] Strong's Greek: #1793. ἐντυγχάνω (entugchanó). From 1722 and 5177; to entreat (in favor or against): deal with, make intercession. "To make petition." Is used of the "pleading" of Elijah against Israel, Romans 11:2, [Revised Standard Version (RSV)], "pleadeth with" (KJV, "maketh intercession to").

it is to plead the blood. Regrettably, the songs have become mere words without real significance! Other than hearing these songs, pleading the blood seldom is mentioned, taught, and, without a doubt, is misunderstood in Christendom.

We must realize that we need to have faith in the precious blood of Jesus Christ—the power of the blood sealed Jesus Christ's victory at Calvary! It is simply not enough to repeat the rhetoric or say the words, "I plead the blood." We need to believe something happens when we plead the blood. The blood of Jesus Christ purges, protects, delivers, speaks for us, and commands victories and deliverance for us—the blood is always victorious! Pleading the blood of Jesus Christ, without a doubt, is a mighty spiritual warfare weapon. Why? It slaps Satan and his forces of darkness right in the face, reminding them of the precious blood's victorious power.

Foundation for Pleading the Blood of Jesus Christ

The concept of pleading the blood of Jesus Christ is rooted in Pentecostal tradition, a necessary tradition and important to continue to invoke, especially in spiritual warfare against Satan and his demonic forces of darkness.

It is very important to note that pleading the blood is not found anywhere in Scripture. Therefore, it is not readily taught. Subsequently, due to a lack of understanding and misconception, many believers do not plead the blood of Jesus Christ. However, the practice of applying the blood is deeply rooted in the Old Testament, where we witness the high priest yearly applied the blood sacrifice of an unblemished lamb to cover the sins of the people.

Additionally, we can trace the pleading of the blood to the Passover. The Passover serves as our focal point to comprehend the power of the blood.

> *And the blood shall be to you for a token upon the houses where ye are: and when I see the blood, I will pass over you, and the plague shall not be upon you to destroy you, when I smite the land of Egypt (Exodus 12:13).*

Exodus 12:13 is very important to our understanding of pleading the blood. The blood was the token of obedience to Jehovah. By this blood sign, with the marking of the blood of the lamb on the doorposts, even the death angel knew which houses to spare or pass over when slaying the firstborn. Faith in Jehovah, His token, and promise provided peace in the houses where the Israelites sprinkled blood in obedience to God's demands.

This Scripture clearly shows us that God saw the blood applied and all conditions met, so He gave security to that home. Doubting by the occupants of the house might destroy the peace, but not the security because it was founded on God's Word. But faith in security without the blood applied would not have brought any, regardless of the personal feelings in the matter. So, it is in the gospel program that all conditions must be met. Repentance must be sincere and accompanied by turning away from sin before there is security in Jesus Christ. A person is not secure in Him while living in sin and when the terms of repentance and living free from sin are not met.[60]

In comparison, 1 Corinthians 5:7 tells us God sacrificed Jesus Christ as our Passover lamb. Therefore, Jesus Christ is the real lamb for our Passover, whereas, in Exodus 12:13, we have the shadow of the lamb of God.

> *Purge out therefore the old leaven, that ye may be a new lump, as ye are unleavened. For even Christ our passover is sacrificed for us* (1 Cor. 5:7).

Furthermore, in Ezekiel 38:14–23, even though the enemy made a formidable descent upon the land of Israel, Israel nevertheless dwelled safely under God's divine protection. Verse 22 gives us a clue why.

> *And I will plead against him with pestilence and with blood; and I will rain upon him, and upon his bands, and upon the many people that are with him, an overflowing rain, and great hailstones, fire, and brimstone* (Ezek. 38:22).

---

[60] Dake, Finis, Jennings, *Dake's Annotated Reference Bible* (Ninth Printing edition), (Lawrenceville: Dake Publishing, Inc, 2006), 121, notes c and *d.

*"And I will **plead** against him with pestilence and **with blood**"* illustrates that when we plead the blood, the promises of security are treasured in the Word of God against troubles and dangers.

Similarly, in Zechariah 9:6–17, we are told to turn to our stronghold, which is the Lord Himself, who is declared to be the stronghold of His people in the day of trouble. This is a reason why we should plead the blood of Jesus Christ in spiritual warfare! Especially note what happens in verses 14 to 16 when we plead the blood.

> **And the Lord shall be seen over them, and his arrow shall go forth as the lightning:** *and the Lord God shall blow the trumpet, and shall go with whirlwinds of the south* (Zech. 9:14, emphasis added).

> **The Lord of hosts shall defend them; and they shall devour,** *and subdue with sling stones; and they shall drink, and make a noise as through wine; and they shall be filled like bowls, and as the corners of the altar* (Zech. 9:15, emphasis added).

> **And the Lord their God shall save them** *in that day as the flock of his people: for they shall be as the stones of a crown, lifted up as an ensign upon his land* (Zech. 9:16).

Verse 14: **"And the Lord shall be seen over them."** In Egypt during the plague, the Word says *"when I see the blood, I will pass over you."* Therefore, the blood of the Lamb becomes a protective presence over us. Indeed, God's presence covers us up in the blood of the Lamb!

Verse 14: **"And his arrow shall go forth as the lightning."** This is what the blood becomes, a spiritual arrow to devour the enemies' camp! The precious blood of Jesus Christ is not just a defensive spiritual weapon but an offensive one as well!

Verse 15: **"The Lord of hosts shall defend them; and they shall devour."** The blood also becomes our defense, and we will devour and subdue our enemies. In fact, Psalm 59:13 tells us the blood consumes our enemies until they are not anymore and the blood lets our enemies know God rules and is in control.

> *Consume them in wrath, consume them, that they may not be: and let them know that God ruleth in Jacob unto the ends of the earth. Selah* (Ps. 59:13).

Verse 16: **"And the Lord their God shall save them."** Ultimately, the Lord Himself becomes our salvation, and we are an ensign[61] in the land.

---

[61] The ensign refers to a standard or a banner around which the nations shall rally. The Messiah Himself will be the rallying point of all nations. To Him they will come and in Him they will put their trust.

> *And he shall set up an ensign for the nations,*
> *and shall assemble the outcasts of Israel, and*
> *gather together the dispersed of Judah from the*
> *four corners of the earth* (Isa. 11:12).

Also, we witness the practice of applying the blood of Jesus Christ in the New Testament. In Revelation 12:7, 8, 11, when there was war in heaven, Michael and his angels fought against and overcame the dragon (Satan) and his angels by the blood of the Lamb.

> *And there was war in heaven: Michael and*
> *his angels fought against the dragon; and the*
> *dragon fought and his angels* (Rev. 12:7).

> *And prevailed not; neither was their place*
> *found any more in heaven* (Rev. 12:8).

> *And they overcame him by the blood of the*
> *Lamb, and by the word of their testimony;*
> *and they loved not their lives unto the death*
> (Rev. 12:11).

What Is Pleading the Blood of Jesus Christ?

Let's examine. What is pleading the blood of Jesus Christ? Pleading the blood activates what happened through the shed blood of Jesus Christ at the cross when He *drenched, blood-bought, blood-stained, and blood-washed* us in His precious blood. When we plead the blood, we ask God to provide what Jesus Christ's blood has already purchased, the great exchange provided by Jesus Christ, and it is at the cross Jesus Christ offered us the most amazing deal in eternity.[62] In essence, pleading the blood of Jesus Christ is a statement of faith about what happened at Calvary and at the cross.

Pleading the blood of Jesus Christ is not the superstitious application of a magic formula of words. It is extremely important for us to understand the reason for the words we use so they do not become a formula. Otherwise, one of two things will happen. First, either what we say becomes a superstitious exercise in which we depend on the words rather than understand what gives the words their power, or second, some people will not plead the blood of Jesus Christ because they do not comprehend the spiritual dynamic, leaving them without a powerful spiritual resource they need.

To preclude this phenomenon from happening, understand when we plead the blood of Jesus Christ, we activate the life and power of God in our midst. When we plead the blood over a situation, a spiritual dynamic is applied because we recognize the victory of Jesus Christ by shedding His precious blood at the cross. A spiritual dynamic is the power of God to do His work. This is exactly what pleading the blood of Jesus Christ is all about. When we plead the blood of Jesus Christ, we are not running from anything, indeed we

---

[62] Chapter 5 *At The Cross*

are always running almost breathlessly to becoming someone who God can fill with His power to attack the devil and his kingdom of darkness.

Jesus Christ's blood is far greater than both the energy of our own humanity and our adversary. The saving power of Jesus Christ's blood is also the same wonderful power that releases, delivers, and neutralizes the enterprises of hell and the weaknesses of our own flesh.

The appropriation of the power of Jesus Christ's blood in tough situations is intended for every believer in Jesus Christ to know, understand, and employ. As born-again believers, we need to value what the blood of Jesus Christ represents and proclaim the power of His blood because it rescued us from death to life when Jesus Christ sacrificed His life as the Lamb of God for us.

We must first realize that pleading the blood of Jesus Christ is a heaven-given spiritual resource that grants us dominion over the works of hell. Consider pleading the blood as a legal defense. We can plead the blood in the same manner an attorney stands before the court and makes a plea on legal grounds, based upon a body of evidence. 1 Samuel 24:15 and Psalm 43:1 help illustrate this point. Note both Scriptures ask God to judge and, as an attorney, to plead my cause against the ungodly.

> *The Lord therefore be judge, and judge between me and thee, and see, and plead my cause, and deliver me out of thine hand* (1 Sam. 24:15).

> *Judge me, O God, and plead my cause against*
> *an ungodly nation: O deliver me from the*
> *deceitful and unjust man* (Ps. 43:1).

When we come before the courts of heaven—and in every circumstance we face in life—we have the legal right, through the blood of Jesus Christ, *drenched in the blood, blood bought, blood washed, and blood stained,* to enter a plea and lay claim to the body of evidence (Jesus Christ's slain body, His shed blood at the cross), which is proven to neutralize the power of sin, affliction, death, and hell.

The blood of Jesus Christ is our spiritual warfare weapon against the enemy and victory over demons. The blood of Jesus Christ entitles us to use His precious blood as an offensive weapon against any adversity that may come our way. This occurred at the cross when Jesus Christ died for our sins. It was at the cross that Jesus Christ defeated Satan and all the powers of darkness.[63]

Subsequently, we must comprehend that when we plead the blood, it reminds Satan he is a defeated foe. It also tells him we are children of God, it is a way to exercise the authority of Jesus Christ over the spirit world and announce to the forces of darkness they are powerless.

When we plead the blood with conviction, the blood of Jesus Christ surrounds us. It is as if we put up a "Do Not Trespass" sign that declares, "Satan, you cannot come, and

---

[63] Suggested for further reading: Colossians 1:13; 2:15, Hebrews 2:14, 1 John 3:8 and Revelation 12:11

you do not have any authority here." Satan may continue to roar as a lion but knows he cannot devour you nor cross the blood of the Lamb who surrounds you.

> *Be sober, be vigilant; because your adversary*
> *the devil, as a roaring lion, walketh about,*
> *seeking whom he may devour* (1 Pet. 5:8).

The blood of Jesus Christ, the Lamb of God, needs to cover every aspect of our lives. Think of pleading the blood of Jesus Christ, if you will, as a counteragent to all Satan tries to throw at us. The blood of Jesus Christ makes it possible for us to defeat the devil on every front! Put another way, you are drenched in the blood of Jesus Christ. Tap into it and flow in its drenching. Realize there's an anointing born out of adversity that throws off anything hell sends your way.

There is not a life circumstance to which the blood of Jesus Christ is not key to God's releasing, protecting, or resolving power, whether it's removing the potential of confusion, overcoming the impact of rebellion, or breaking the torment of fear or the shame of the past. When we plead the blood of Jesus Christ, we do so with supernatural firepower and on the basis of the body of evidence that, through the blood of Jesus Christ, we gained victory over Satan and his forces of darkness, all sin neutralized, the power of death overwhelmed and every human need paid for once and for all.

Why Plead the Blood of Jesus Christ?

Let us investigate why we should plead the blood of Jesus Christ. First, there is power in the blood of the Lamb, but the power is useless if we neglect to use it. Everything we believe, teach, and hope for is intimately tied to the power of the blood of the Lamb—Jesus Christ. As believers, we have the right to declare and plead the blood of Jesus Christ because His blood redeemed and purchased us. The blood of Jesus Christ supersedes all attacks, afflictions, and temptations.

Second, we must appreciate Jesus Christ's precious blood is the greatest spiritual warfare weapon against Satan and his forces of darkness. The blood of Jesus Christ is more than a vital part of our salvation and is meant for us to use both offensively and defensively as a spiritual warfare weapon. Subsequently, we need to learn how to activate, walk, and flow in the power of Jesus Christ's precious blood in our daily lives.

Third, pleading the blood establishes legal authority over and around us. Satan and his forces of darkness understand this legal authority and are forced to obey it. When we plead the blood of Jesus Christ, we establish a legal boundary and vested interest. Understand wherever we have a vested interest, like our home or land, family and loved ones, or job, we can establish legal authority over it. That is done by placing it under the authority of the blood. When we plead the blood, it gives us the legal spiritual authority over all evil that tries to come against our vested interest.

Protection and deliverance are two major reasons why we should plead the blood of Jesus Christ. In times of physical and spiritual attack and in threatening situations of any kind, those who trust in the Lord find Him to be a strong Protector. "He shields all who take refuge in Him" (Psalm 18:30). Protection is when we plead the blood of Jesus Christ over whatever we want God to shield before any attacks or adversity could strike them, such as our body, soul, house, and finances. As believers, we must go on the offensive in spiritual warfare by daily pleading the blood to protect us from enemy attacks.

The Passover is the greatest principle to illustrate how pleading the blood does this. As we noted in Exodus 12:13, the Israelites were protected from the angel of death when they smeared the first Passover lambs' blood on their doorposts. In comparison, as we saw in 1 Corinthians 5:7, our Passover Lamb, Jesus Christ, who was sacrificed for us, did the same with His precious blood, protecting us now and into eternity.

When we plead the blood of Jesus Christ because we have been attacked by some kind of adversity and now need God's healing power to free us, we receive deliverance. We must learn to plead the blood of Jesus Christ for deliverance and provision in the courts of heaven. His sacred blood is far better than any sacrifice we could offer. Jesus Christ's precious blood speaks on our behalf, declaring, "Justice is satisfied, freedom is granted and provision is released!"

Jesus Christ drenched us in His blood and He *bloodbought, blood-stained, and blood-washed* us so we can experience the power, authority, and deliverance of His blood. We see this phenomenon of deliverance due to the blood of Jesus Christ over the power of darkness, the power of death, the wrestling against principalities, powers, world rulers of darkness, and spiritual wickedness in a high place, and it destroys the works of the devil and helps us overcome.

Power over Darkness

Colossians 1:13–14 inform us Jesus Christ delivered us from Satan, his power and kingdom of sin, sickness, and depravity to place us under the government of the Son of God's love. Redemption through Jesus Christ's precious blood made this possible.[64]

> *Who hath delivered us from the power of darkness, and hath translated us into the kingdom of his dear Son. In whom we have redemption through his blood, even the forgiveness of sins* (Col. 1:13–14).

---

[64] Dake, Finis, Jennings, *Dake's Annotated Reference Bible* (Ninth Printing edition), (Lawrenceville: Dake Publishing, Inc, 2006), 384, note m.

Power over Death

Satan was conquered. In Genesis 3:15, God the Father promised, "*And I will put enmity between thee and the woman, and between thy seed and her seed; it shall bruise thy head, and thou shalt bruise his heel.*" In comparison, Hebrews 2:14 states, "*Forasmuch then as the children are partakers of flesh and blood, he also himself likewise took part of the same; that through death he might destroy him that had the power of death, that is, the devil.*" From these two Scriptures, we learn at a place called Calvary, Jesus Christ conquered sin, death, and satanic principalities in the heavenly places. Jesus Christ's shed blood, death, and resurrection brought victory over all spiritual forces of darkness.

Wrestling Against Spiritual Forces of Evil

We are engaged in ongoing spiritual warfare with unseen spiritual forces of evil. Unfortunately, too many Christians are too passive when any type of severe adversity confronts them. Regrettably, most Christians are not taught how to engage in spiritual warfare or how to go on the offensive when the enemy launches an all-out, full-scale attack against them.

Oftentimes, we witness Christians wrestle against flesh and blood (people). However, Ephesians 6:12 warns us not to wrestle against flesh and blood but against those spiritual forces who are against God. Our warfare is indeed spiritual, not physical. The enemy we wrestle against can never be fought in the natural plain or the physical realm but only in the spiritual realm. Whether we like it or not, we are engaged in spiritual warfare with a wicked fallen angel and many evil principalities, powers, world rulers of darkness, and spiritual wickedness in high places who are the authors of evil, deception, lies, fear, sin, evil, unrest, and war.

It is God Himself who girds us with strength and arms us for spiritual warfare with the precious blood of Jesus Christ. We must appreciate Jesus Christ's blood is the greatest spiritual warfare weapon against Satan and his forces of darkness. Jesus Christ's shed blood, death, and resurrection brought victory over all spiritual forces of darkness.

Understand, if we do not fight and simply stand around or hide from the reality of spiritual warfare or actually run away from it, we are defeated! When this happens, Satan takes us as prisoners of war, and we are simply heaven bound but absolutely not a threat to Satan, our enemy. Consequently, Satan and his satanic kingdom run amuck and unchecked to steal, kill, and destroy!

It is time for Christians to become steadfast, and immovable, and stop running from the battlefield. Instead, run to it armed with the precious blood of Jesus Christ and our God-given authority. When we stand firm in the Lord Jesus Christ, we can live in victory over Satan's schemes. Realize Jesus Christ has all authority (all power of absolute rule) in heaven and on earth and gives us this authority. So run to the battlefield and exercise the authority and power[65] Jesus Christ gives us.

> *And when he had called unto him his twelve disciples, he gave them power against unclean spirits, to cast them out, and to heal all manner of sickness and all manner of disease* (Matt. 10:1).

> *And Jesus came and spake unto them, saying, All power is given unto me in heaven and in earth* (Matt. 28:18).

> *Then he called his twelve disciples together, and gave them power and authority over all devils, and to cure diseases* (Luke 9:1).

> *Behold, I give unto you power to tread on serpents and scorpions, and over all the power of the enemy: and nothing shall by any means hurt you* (Luke 10:19).

---

[65] Authority is the right to rule, command and make decisions. Authority is the channel through which power operates. Whereas, power is the ability/capacity to influence the beliefs, actions or behavior of others. While power is ability in general, authority can be summed up by the word "control" or "rule."

Understand by our position in Jesus Christ and the Holy Spirit dwelling in us that we have far more authority and power than Satan and his satanic kingdom. Unfortunately, some Christians fail to comprehend their God-given authority gives them the right to use the power Jesus Christ gives them through the indwelling of God's Holy Spirit.

> *And if children, then heirs; heirs of God, and joint-heirs with Christ; if so be that we suffer with him, that we may be also glorified together* (Rom. 8:17).

> *Nay, in all these things we are more than conquerors through him that loved us* (Rom. 8:37).

> *Wherefore thou art no more a servant, but a son; and if a son, then an heir of God through Christ* (Gal. 4:7).

> *Ye are of God, little children, and have overcome them: because greater is he that is in you, than he that is in the world* (1 John 4:4).

We would do well to consider when the Holy Spirit dwells in us, we are invested with the power of God Himself and the full authority of Jesus Christ to use it. What a tragedy that many of God's chosen people, although given both Jesus

Christ's authority and power, do not realize what is theirs or refuse to exercise those rights.[66]

Realize we assume our God-given authority on the battlefield and it is Satan and his forces of darkness we pursue and challenge when we exercise that authority. Let's examine some ways, we, as Christians, can assert our authority.

Align Our Will With God's

Every Christian should have confidence in God and realize He promises us the right to use our God-given authority to manifest whatsoever we ask in accordance with His will (1 John 5:14). What we have to do is align our will with God's. Then assert the authority God gave us. Realize God gives us authority because He wants us to challenge the enemy's forces in Jesus Christ's name and push back against Satan's kingdom.

Power of a Decree

The power of a decree is another way we assert our authority on the battlefield. A decree is an order usually having the force of law (Merriam-Webster Dictionary). According to Jennifer LeClaire, "I power of a decree is nothing new. It's an ancient principle for establishing law in the spirit realm that

---

[66] *If Only We Realized How Much Power We Carry!* Kraft, Charles H, *I Give You Authority,* (Grand Rapids: Chosen Books, A Division of Baker Book House Company, 2000), 63.

even secular kings and rulers translated to the natural realm."[67] We must realize God, the Father, takes decrees seriously and so should we!

> *Ye shall do my judgments, and keep mine ordinances, to walk therein: I am the Lord your God* (Lev. 18:4).

> *Wherefore ye shall do my statutes, and **keep my judgments, and do them**; and ye shall dwell in the land in safety* (Lev. 25:18, emphasis added).

We can decree the Word of God or His revealed will in our battle against Satan's kingdom of darkness to bring God's Kingdom about. Every believer in Jesus Christ will encounter spiritual warfare and Jesus Christ illustrates how to defeat Satan by decreeing God's Word. In Luke 4:1-13, we witness that after Jesus Christ was filled with the Holy Spirit, He immediately engaged in spiritual warfare. Through a series of temptations that appealed to His weakness, desire, and pride, Satan came to contest the territory Jesus Christ had won. Note in each instance, Jesus Christ won the victory against the devil by decreeing and standing on the Word of God and He answered Satan, saying

---

[67] LeClaire, Jennifer, *Decrees That Make the Devil Flee,* (Fort Lauderdale: Awakening Media, 2020), 5.

> ***It is written, That man shall not live by bread alone, but by every word of God*** (Luke 4:4, emphasis added)

> ***Get thee behind me, Satan: for it is written,*** *Thou shalt worship the Lord thy God, and him only shalt thou serve* (Luke 4:8, emphasis added)

> *It is said,* ***Thou shalt not tempt the Lord thy God*** (Luke 4:12, emphasis added)

As long as we align with and decree God's will and His Word, the enemy is bound to obey.

Why?

Decrees release judgement against the enemy and establish the will of the Lord. Therefore, remember when the enemy confronts you with evil in your life, a decree can release God's judgement and restore your future and hope. If we do not assert our authority over Satan, he will assert his authority over us.

On the other hand, every time we assert our authority on the battlefield, we enlarge our steps into the domain of darkness, destroy the works of Satan, and the God of peace shall bruise (crush) Satan under our feet. Therefore, do not give Satan time to talk you out of the fight. Do not shrink back from the fight. Engage these spiritual forces of darkness and plead the blood of Jesus Christ against them!

Destroys the works of the devil

As mentioned in Chapter 5, it is at the cross that Jesus Christ destroyed the twenty-five works of the devil.

> *He that committeth sin is of the devil; for the devil sinneth from the beginning. For this purpose the Son of God was manifested, that he might destroy the works of the devil* (1 John 3:8).

Helps us overcome Satan

Revelation 12:11 tells us we overcame Satan because of the blood of the Lamb and the word of our testimony.

> *And they overcame him by the blood of the Lamb, and by the word of their testimony; and they loved not their lives unto the death* (Rev. 12:11).

God gave us the blood of Jesus Christ as a wonderful spiritual weapon, shield, and hiding place to use. Regardless of how the enemy comes, whether in discouragement, temptation, sickness, or any other way, the blood of the Lamb and the word of our testimony overcome the enemy—the shed blood of Jesus Christ gives us power over Satan!

We must be aware Satan is God's enemy and our accuser. The accusation against the brethren is one of Satan's primary weapons against us. Day and night, Satan points out our failures and accuses us of sin. Satan's goal is to weaken and even paralyze us. He wants to cheat us of our relationship with God and what the Lord Jesus Christ has done for us. This is where the blood of Jesus Christ becomes infinitely precious when we engage in spiritual warfare.

> *And I heard a loud voice saying in heaven, Now is come salvation, and strength, and the kingdom of our God, and the power of his Christ: for the accuser of our brethren is cast down, which accused them before our God day and night* (Rev. 12:10).

It is the blood of Jesus Christ that paid the price for and blotted out our sins. Therefore, the blood of Jesus Christ sets us free, and we do not any longer have to listen to the accusations Satan hurls day and night. Realize Jesus Christ provided victory for us over Satan through His precious blood. Hence, when Satan's demons come against us, we must clearly understand the blood of Jesus Christ satisfied every charge Satan can levy against us. Furthermore, the blood of Jesus Christ accomplished four things for us:[68]

1. The blood unites us in fellowship with the Father.
2. The blood gives us the power to defeat the forces of darkness.
3. The blood gives us power over our own sinful nature.
4. The blood establishes an unassailable bond with a sovereign God that prevents Satan from separating the embattled Christian from God's eternal and complete resources.

Satan does not have any legal footing in the courts of heaven. This is why pleading the blood of Jesus Christ is vitally important as well as a powerful spiritual weapon. When we plead the blood, we publicly affirm our God-given freedom from the guilt and condemnation of sin and its judgment. This leaves Satan speechless in God's holy presence and the courts of heaven.

Additionally, Jesus Christ's shed blood brought victory over Satan and his spiritual forces of darkness. When we plead the blood of Jesus Christ, we surround ourselves with His precious blood and release the very power and authority of Jesus Christ over what we plead the blood over and against. Understand, we need to plead the blood of Jesus Christ

---

[68] *Kingdom Dynamics Note,* Hayford, Jack, *Spirit Filled Life Bible for Students,* New King James Version, (Nashville: Thomas Nelson Publishers, 1982), 1683.

whenever we sense the accusation of Satan and refer Satan, the one who accuses us, to the blood of the Lamb.

Instead of succumbing to Satan's accusations, we must reject them. When he accuses, simply declare, *"Satan, I reject your accusations. Look at the blood of Jesus Christ. God is satisfied by Jesus Christ's redeeming blood, my conscience is purified with His cleansing blood, and you're defeated by His overcoming blood!"*

The blood of Jesus Christ always overcomes the enemy. It might take time, but it always overcomes. This is especially true when we first plead the blood of Jesus Christ. However, as our revelation in the power of the blood increases, so will the authority of Jesus Christ available to us increase – continuously and persistently pleading for the blood is very important in spiritual warfare!

It behooves us to constantly remember that as we plead the blood of Jesus Christ, it contends and protects us from the powers of darkness. The blood also speaks on our behalf. As we read in chapter 1, Jesus Christ's blood speaks better things than Abel's blood, which cried out for vengeance. Jesus Christ's blood speaks of our rights in Christ— the forgiveness of sins and Satan's defeat.

What Pleading the Blood of Jesus Christ Is Not

Let's examine what pleading the blood of Jesus Christ is not and then shift our focus to what pleading the blood is. Begging for what we want is a common misconception surrounding pleading the blood of Jesus Christ. Realize when we speak about pleading the blood of Jesus Christ, we are not talking about begging God to do something. We should not plead the blood in selfish and negative ways, especially when thinking we have the power through these words to make God give us something. Subsequently, we should not consider pleading the blood of Jesus Christ as an entitlement for whatever we want and as a desperation exercise because God has not called us to beg before Him. Also, pleading the blood is not a statement of unbelief or fear.

Criteria for Pleading the Blood of Jesus Christ

Being saved and surrendered are two fundamental criteria we must meet to effectively plead the blood of Jesus Christ for any kind of protection and deliverance we may need. It should not surprise us that a nonbeliever cannot use the blood of Jesus Christ. As we noted in Exodus 12:13, only God's chosen people were allowed to apply the blood of the lamb on their doorposts for protection. It is the same way in the New Testament. Only born-again, Christian believers can use the blood of Jesus Christ for protection and deliverance.

Though we are saved and born-again Christians, when we plead the blood, surrendering is the other fundamental criterion we must meet to receive God's maximum protection. At this juncture in your walk with Jesus Christ, you must decide who will control the rest of your life from now on, you or God.

Spiritual reality dictates we should be controlled/influenced by the Holy Spirit – not robotically but led and empowered.

When you turn your life over to the Lord for Him to completely handle, your life will propel you along a completely different path (guided by God) versus the one your life would take if you decide to maintain control and not let go and let God. Realize when you maintain control, you live in your own capacity—your flesh, thoughts, limits, and power—until you let go and let God. Only then will you live in God's capacity beyond your limits, power, and capacity.

A word of caution before you decide to surrender to God fully and completely. You must think about the ramifications of what full and complete surrender entails. Without a doubt, this is a life-altering decision. You must realize you should not entertain the thought of turning back when you fully and completely surrender to God. Jesus Christ tells us in Luke 9:62 that anyone who puts their hand to the plow and looks back is not fit for the kingdom of God.

Why do we need to surrender to God? Essentially, God fearfully and wonderfully made us to have a personal, intimate relationship with Him. The only way to do this, on our part, is to give God our whole hearts through surrender, laying our lives down for Him. We must come to a place of abiding in Jesus Christ without wavering and without any obstacle to the flow of God's Spirit in our lives. When we reach this place of deep intimacy and surrender to God, we experience, at a level we never dreamed possible, the joy, peace, and overflowing sense of love that we long for.

Though life is hard and challenging at times, we need to firmly believe God has the best in mind for us. God has a perfect plan and destiny for us and will lead us on the absolute best path for our lives. God's plan for our lives does not change even though our life may take turns we never expected. God loves us enough to plan for our future and actively involves Himself in all that concerns us. In fact, in the below passages, we witness:

> *Shew me thy ways, O Lord; teach me thy paths* (Ps. 25:4).

> *Teach me thy way, O Lord, and lead me in a plain path, because of mine enemies* (Ps. 27:11).

God has a vested interest in the plan for our lives, which is why He instructs, teaches, and guides us in the way we should go.

> *I will instruct thee and teach thee in the way which thou shalt go: I will guide thee with mine eye* (Ps. 32:8).

In Jeremiah 29:11, God says *"For I know the thoughts that I think toward you, thoughts of peace and not of evil, to give you an expected end."* We must see ourselves as God sees us, as a Father who loves His beloved, blood-bought child who needs His divine guidance to navigate life's challenges. Once we surrender, God will guide our steps along a specific path, especially through life challenges and difficulties, to give us an expected end-all for His glory. So, when we surrender to God, we basically tell Him we trust Him and the plan He has for us.

Everything is subject to God's plan for your life as you obey Him inch by inch. Our heavenly Father has the best plan for your life and has equipped you and provided provisions for you to accomplish His plan. Fix your thoughts on Jesus Christ and take hold of God's plan.

Understand God has a divine plan for your life. He devised and tailored this plan specifically with you in mind. God took just as much care and attention when He formed you as when He draws you into intimacy with Him. God's design encompasses your physical qualities and comprises the spiritual realm of how we grow in our faith and character.

God also empowered you to fulfill His purpose and destiny He preordained for your life as you walk with Him. That means you should willingly submit your own desires to the Father to do His will. As long as you trust and continually seek God, He will never leave you wondering what He desires of you. In fact, when you seek and draw nigh to God, He will draw nigh to you so that you remain connected to Him through an intimate relationship.

Surrender your body, soul, spirit, will, and entire life to God because, in God, all things are made new. Your greatest desire should be for God to keep you in the center of His plan. It is the Lord who not only directs our path but also shapes and molds our hearts and characters to align with His plan.

God is also fully invested in His entire plan for each one of us. Therefore, follow God forward in His plan. He will direct you through the fog and lead you step by step and from glory to glory. So, stop fighting God for control and trust His all-powerful, all-knowing, and unconditionally loving plan!

The passages below affirm God is the one who directs our steps. Furthermore, these Scriptures tell us our lives do not belong to us, are not our own to control, nor are we able to direct our steps as we walk, and without God, our best laid plans (based on human thoughts and emotions) will undoubtedly end in failure and ruin.

> *A man's heart deviseth his way: but the Lord directeth his steps* (Prov. 16:9).

> *O Lord, I know that the way of man is not in himself: it is not in man that walketh to direct his steps* (Jer. 10:23).

God has a perfect divine plan, purpose, and destiny for your life. When you let go and let God, as indicated in the below Scriptures, He will direct your steps in life and guide you every step of the way into the fulfillment of His divine plan.

> *But I trusted in thee, O Lord: I said, Thou art my God. My times are in thy hand: deliver me*

from the hand of mine enemies, and from them that persecute me (Ps. 31:14–15).

I will instruct thee and teach thee in the way which thou shalt go: I will guide thee with mine eye (Ps. 32:8).

Delight thyself also in the Lord: and he shall give thee the desires of thine heart. Commit thy way unto the Lord; trust also in him; and he shall bring it to pass. And he shall bring forth thy righteousness as the light, and thy judgment as the noonday. Rest in the Lord, and wait patiently for him: fret not thyself because of him who prospereth in his way, because of the man who bringeth wicked devices to pass (Ps. 37:4–7).

The steps of a good man are ordered by the Lord: and he delighteth in his way (Ps. 37:23).

For this God is our God for ever and ever: he will be our guide even unto death (Ps. 48:14).

Order my steps in thy word: and let not any iniquity have dominion over me (Ps. 119:133).

Thine eyes did see my substance, yet being unperfect; and in thy book all my members were written, which in continuance were fashioned, when as yet there was none of them (Ps. 139:16).

Trust in the Lord with all thine heart; and lean not unto thine own understanding. In all thy ways acknowledge him, and he shall direct thy paths. Be not wise in thine own eyes: fear the Lord, and depart from evil. It shall be health to thy navel, and marrow to thy bones (Prov. 3:5–8).

There is a way which seemeth right unto a man, but the end thereof are the ways of death (Prov. 14:12).

Commit thy works unto the Lord, and thy thoughts shall be established (Prov. 16:3).

Man's goings are of the Lord; how can a man then understand his own way (Prov. 20:24)?

Thus saith the Lord, thy Redeemer, the Holy One of Israel; I am the Lord thy God which teacheth thee to profit, which leadeth thee by the way that thou shouldest go (Isa. 48:17).

*And the Lord shall guide thee continually, and
satisfy thy soul in drought, and make fat thy
bones: and thou shalt be like a watered garden,
and like a spring of water, whose waters fail not*
(Isa. 58:11).

Realize as long as we try to devise a solution, we will miss
God's solution and what God is doing. Instead, cease your
efforts and simply trust in the Lord. God is not asking you to
figure out His plan, just believe Him, submit to, surrender to,
believe in, and trust in His plan. Once we do this, set Your
heart to hear and obey what God is saying and He will reveal
His plan to you.

God's earnest desire is to show us His plan when we seek
and trust Him. Make not any mistake about this, it is God's
character to reveal Himself and His will to us. Realize God
wants us to walk along a particular path and will show us His
ways and teach us His paths. In fact, God will not let our feet
stagger when we closely walk His paths. In other words, God
will reach out to take our hands in His strong right hand to
lead and cause us to walk on a straight (smooth/uncluttered)
path in which we will not stumble. Likewise, when we submit,
God must assume responsibility for leading, instructing, and
guiding us along His path.

*Hold up my goings in thy paths, that my foot-
steps slip not* (Ps. 17:5).

He will not suffer thy foot to be moved: he that keepeth thee will not slumber (Ps. 121:3).

Then shalt thou walk in thy way safely, and thy foot shall not stumble (Prov. 3:23).

God knows from our limited, earthly perspective that the path can become confusing, and the choices we face are difficult and complex, to say the least. But as a loving and faithful Father, God, who sees perfectly what is ahead as well as what we require to face the challenge, He is more than willing to help, instruct, teach, arm us with strength, and make our way perfect. The passages below provide us with this assurance.

It is God that girdeth me with strength, and maketh my way perfect (Ps. 18:32).

I will instruct thee and teach thee in the way which thou shalt go: I will guide thee with mine eye (Ps. 32:8).

God will direct your path in ways beyond your imagination—exceedingly, abundantly above all that you can ask or think. God's plan gives you an expected end and positions you for an open door of purpose, destiny, and blessing.

Surrender control to God and firmly fix your heart and focus on Jesus Christ, drawing nearer to Him spiritually, relationally, emotionally, intellectually, physically, and psychologically. Then stand back and watch God take care of the rest. This, however, only comes through the surrender of our hearts. If surrendering is to give up, the Lord says we need to give up our thoughts and ways for His thoughts and ways.

The process of surrender is constant and not a one-time event. Surrender softens our hearts and positions us to hear from the Lord, whether we like what He says or not. As we surrender to God, laying our lives down, totally trusting, depending, and fixing our eyes firmly on Jesus Christ, a greater heartfelt desire to seek the kingdom of God first and His righteousness develops. This causes us to do God's will with boldness and confidence that impact lives and glorify God. That is why we need to surrender our will and way of doing things for His will and His way of doing things!

You must willingly, fully, and completely surrender your entire being, body, soul, spirit, will, and entire life to God the Father. You must submit yourself to God and tell Him you trust Him to show you what to do, step by step, and remember we can do all things through Christ who strengthens us (Philippians 4:13). We do not need the whole plan right now. When God instructs you to step forward, just obey Him.

Go forward in faith and totally trust God. Realize God knows exactly what we need, what we can handle, and when we need it. God factored all this into His divine plan for you. Therefore, do not take shortcuts around God's planned route for you. Oftentimes, we either get tired of waiting for God and rush ahead of Him or go in an entirely different direction. However, timing is everything to God! Understand God will not alter His mind nor His plan for you—He has spiritual maturity, training, and blessings He wants you to enjoy.

Subsequently, that is why it is extremely important to trust God to lead us—keep pressing forward even when you encounter growing pains. Just embrace and trust His plan. Ultimately, God provides what we most long for—His leadership into a bright, fulfilling future.

> *Ye shall walk in all the ways which the Lord your God hath commanded you, that ye may live, and that it may be well with you, and that ye may prolong your days in the land which ye shall possess* (Deut. 5:33).

Fix your eyes on Jesus Christ, take a deep breath, relax and let Him lead. When you do this, the devil will flee (James 4:7). Understand, when we fix our eyes on Jesus Christ, regardless of the circumstance or problem, we show Jesus Christ, we trust Him and look to Him alone for help.

First Thessalonians 5:23 informs us we are triune beings made up of three parts: body, soul, and spirit. God wants our full and complete surrender in all three parts. When we do this, the best of God flows in our lives.

Unfortunately, this full and complete surrender to God is where many Christians miss the boat with Him. They are saved through grace by the blood of Jesus Christ but do not walk in this full and complete surrender to God the Father.

As a result, they do not see God's full force working in and through their lives.

Regrettably, this lack of full and complete surrender to God the Father plays havoc in the lives of so many Christians. They do not have God's full protection on them and come under severe attacks from Satan and the forces of darkness.

At this point, you have probably said to yourself, this is all well and good, but how do I fully and completely surrender my body, soul, spirit, will, and entire life to God? Let us explore two ways. Let go and let God place our bodies before God as a living sacrifice and continually renew our minds in Jesus Christ.

The First Way to Surrender to God is to Let Go and Let God Take Control.[69]

One of the hardest things for us to bear is not having control over our own circumstances. However, this is exactly how Jesus Christ calls us to live. Luke 9:23–24 makes it plain that anyone who intends to come after Jesus Christ has to let Him lead. We are not in the driver's seat; Jesus Christ is! He is now our Lord and Master and we do not any longer have the right to rule over ourselves.

---

[69] Six bible verses "to let go and let God": Exodus 14:14 – The Lord fights for you, 2 Chronicles 15:7 – Be strong and do not give up, Psalm 34:17 – God delivers the righteous from all their troubles, Proverbs 16:3 – Commit your works unto the Lord, Song of Songs 4:7 – You are altogether beautiful and there is not any flaw in you and 1 Peter 5:7- Cast your care on the Lord.

And he said to them all, If any man will come after me, let him deny himself, and take up his cross daily, and follow me. For whosoever will save his life shall lose it: but whosoever will lose his life for my sake, the same shall save it (Luke 9:23–24).

To let go and let God is an ongoing moment-by-moment choice, a daily process of trusting God with our lives and choices and keeping our focus on the eternal. When you surrender control, you're welcoming God's will to take the predominant place in your life. You're letting go and trusting God with the rest. Therefore, surrender to God's divine plan. He devised and tailored this plan specifically with you in mind. So just let go and let God!

When you do so, not only will God show you the best road to take, but He will also lead and guide you along the path to an expected end-all for His glory. This is a very important concept to remember. Why? At times we find ourselves at a crossroads and if we do not let go and let God, we will make decisions that will set the course for our lives. Unfortunately, regardless of how vigilant we are, we are still blind to our decisions' significance or impact on us as well as others. Fortunately, when we let go and let God take control, He will always direct us in the right way. Realize God knows the best way to take and how to navigate the obstacles in a manner that will not break your spirit.

> *For thou art my rock and my fortress; there-*
> *fore for thy name's sake lead me, and guide me*
> (Ps. 31:3).

> *There is a way that seemeth right unto a man,*
> *but the end thereof are the ways of death*
> (Prov. 16:25).

Surrender often reveals things in us that need removing and pruning. Therefore, we need to let go of control, stripping away all the things that do not speak of nor reveal God in our lives. Take a moment to examine your life. Are there areas in your life where pruning needs to or is taking place? Ask the Holy Spirit to reveal areas of your life to let go and surrender to God so that you become a child of God who bears fruit. This process isn't easy and can feel very raw, uncomfortable, and revealing.

Surrendering to God is the relinquishing of your rights and submitting your will to God's will. It is surrendering your body, soul, spirit, will, and entire life—thoughts, actions, hopes, dreams, and expectations to God.

It is a matter of doing something God's way and to please Him. Such as, it is a matter of going where God wants you to go and doing what He wants you to do. It is a matter of serving God and committing to do things His way. It is a matter of stopping wrestling with God for control and relinquishing control to Him. Do not continue to struggle with God for control—let it go!

Realize whenever we draw a line in the sand between God, the Father, and ourselves over any issue, regardless of how large or small, we actively choose disappointment, heartache, and ultimately hinder our relationship with God the Father and Jesus Christ the Son.

Nothing pleases the Father more than our full and complete surrender, so let go and let God! It is a matter of opening up that tight-closed fist of control and placing trust in God instead of yourself. It is a matter of realizing that daily giving your life to God changes everything. It is a matter of saying each morning to God:

> *I submit to You, God and resist the devil. I say a quiet yes to You and a loud no to the devil. I surrender my body, my soul, my spirit, my will and my entire life to You. I submit to, surrender to, trust in, walk in, have faith in and believe in your plan. Align my body, my soul, my spirit and my entire life to Your plan. I am Yours, Lord. I exist for Your glory. Lead me by Your Holy Spirit. Cause me to be very sensitive to Your Holy Spirit. Work through me today. Show me how to live for You – acting and thinking as Jesus Christ would. Help me to glorify You today.*

The Second Way to Surrender to God Fully and Completely

We need to place our body before God as a living sacrifice and continually renew our minds in Jesus Christ as recorded in Romans 12:1-2, seek God, come to Him in prayer, and spend time in His Word. Learn and apply His biblical truths and surrender to God's ways and if we do not, we, unfortunately, leave our minds with room for the enemy to cause havoc.

Our thought life is absolutely powerful. Hence, we need to cast down imaginations and every high thing that exalts itself against the knowledge of God and brings into captivity every thought to the obedience of Christ. In other words, take our thoughts captive and do not let them become part of our lives if they are not from the Word of God. Also, we need to take our everyday, ordinary life—our sleeping, eating, and going-to-work and walking-around life—and place it before God as an offering.

Embracing what God does for us is the best thing we can do for God. Do not become so well-adjusted to your culture and conformed to this world that you pattern yourself after it, fitting into it without even thinking. Instead, fix your attention on God. This will change you from the inside out. Readily recognize what He wants from you and quickly respond to it because God only wants to bring the best out of you.

How to Plead the Blood of Jesus Christ

There are some churches that talk about the power of pleading the blood of Jesus Christ. But they do not teach us exactly how to do it, what to plead it on, what to plead it against, and, most importantly, how to plead the blood to receive God's maximum protection and deliverance. So how do we plead the blood of Jesus Christ in prayer? We simply do five things:

Repent of what the Holy Spirit Brings to Mind

1. Repent what the Holy Spirit brings to mind and acknowledge Jesus Christ shed His blood for you as a sinner and established a relationship between you and the Lord. All known sins must be confessed and turned away, and there must not be any unforgiveness in your heart. Any open or hidden sin in our lives (i.e., unforgiveness, disobedience, rebellion, fear, anxiety, doubt, unbelief, and sin) acts as spiritual blocks.

Satan, our adversary, is always making legal pleadings against us to God, using our unconfessed sins (our spiritual blocks) to gain footholds into our lives to destroy us. However, our defense attorney, Jesus Christ, intercedes on our behalf to plead our case before the courts of heaven. Jesus Christ's blood gives us legal standing with God, the judge of the universe, to listen to us and hear our case. One of the first things we must do is to quickly agree with our adversary that we have sinned, then repent immediately before the Lord.

> *Agree with thine adversary quickly, whiles thou art in the way with him; lest at any time the adversary deliver thee to the judge, and the judge deliver thee to the officer, and thou be cast into prison* (Matt. 5:25).

We must quickly realize there is not any need to try to cover or pretty up our sins to God. He already knows everything we have done (1 John 3:20). But be honest with God and acknowledge your sins and transgressions. We can do this by reading, meditating, and praying Psalm 51, a prayer for spiritual cleansing.

Remind the Heavenly Father of His Will

2. Remind the heavenly Father what His will is as revealed in Scripture. We should figure out what God already wants to do and pray for Him to do it. Isaiah 43:26 tells us to put God in remembrance so that we may be justified. When we do this and pray God's words back to Him, we always pray in agreement with God's will, giving God permission to do the things on earth that He wants to do but had to wait until we ask. Since God gave us dominion over the fish of the sea and over the fowl of the air and over every living

thing that moves on the earth (Gen. 1:28) He does not usurp our God-given dominion over the earth. Instead, *the Lord God does nothing without revealing his counsel to his servants the prophets* (Amos 3:7). We come into agreement with His pre-determined plan and purpose for our lives. When we do this, we open the doors for heaven to invade earth in our lives.

> *And this is the confidence that we have in him,*
> *that, if we ask any thing according to his will,*
> *he heareth us* (1 John 5:14).

Understand that the Bible clearly outlines God's will. Every single situation we face or will face in our lives has a solution and an answer (usually more than one) recorded in the Bible. Everything! The Bible says specifically what we should do in every situation, or it contains principles we should apply to ascertain the answers based on God's principles. For example, when we need healing, remind God, *"by His stripes I am healed"* (Isa. 53:5) or *"He is Jehovah-Rapha, the Lord that heals"* (Exod. 15:26). Our body must come into alignment with the perfect healing Jesus Christ's blood paid for us to have.

Remind God of Jesus Christ's Blood

3. Remind God that Jesus Christ poured out His blood on the cross so that God's will would be done.

Remind God to Carry Out His Perfect Will

4. Remind God the Father to carry out His perfect will based on Jesus Christ's precious shed blood, which is the legal currency with which Jesus Christ purchased our victory. Hebrews 10:19–23 also reminds us Jesus Christ's blood was the currency that He poured out (in obedience to the Father), which bought us access to God Himself and unrivaled intimacy with Him, a covenant relationship was made. To plead the blood of Jesus Christ means that we can enter into God's presence, make our requests known, and hear from Him. Because a covenant is made with the Father, we can now—without hesitation—walk right up to God, into the Holy Place because we are drenched with the blood of Jesus Christ. Jesus Christ cleared the way by the blood of His sacrifice, acting as our priest before God. The "curtain" into God's presence is Jesus Christ's crucified body and shed blood.

    Having therefore, brethren, boldness to enter into the holiest by the blood of Jesus, By a new and living way, which he hath consecrated for us, through the veil, that is to say, his flesh; And having an high priest over the house of God; Let us draw near with a true heart in full assurance of faith, having our hearts sprinkled from an evil conscience, and our bodies washed with pure water. Let us hold fast the profession of our

> *faith without wavering (for he is faithful that*
> *promised;)* (Heb. 10:19–23).

When We Plead the Blood of Jesus Christ

5. When we plead the blood of Jesus Christ, we must not
    make blanket pleas to the righteous Judge but be more
    definite with our requests—mention our exact needs and
    align them with Scripture to achieve the desired effective-
    ness. In other words, be specific (people, places, issues,
    and demons)!

GLOSSARY/DEFINITIONS

anointed; anointing; anoints. To smear or rub with oil or an oily substance; to apply oil to as part of a religious ceremony. Source: Merriam-Webster Dictionary.

enmity. The word enmity is from the Greek word "echthra" and means "hate, being hostile with" or "in opposition too." Our sin alienated us from God. Source: https://www.patheos.com/blogs/christiancrier/2015/08/14/what-does-enmity-mean-a-biblical-definition-of-enmity/

decree. An order usually having the force of law. Source: Merriam-Webster Dictionary.

drenched. Completely soaked/saturated. Source: https://biblehub.com/topical/d/drench.htm

Golgotha. The Aramaic name of the location where Jesus Christ was crucified outside of Old Jerusalem. Source: https://www.gotquestions.org/Golgotha-Calvary.html

petition. (Aramaic) or b ah (Aramaic) {beh-aw'}; corresponding to ba'ah; to seek or ask — ask, desire, make (petition), pray, request, seek. Source: Strong's Hebrew/Aramaic # 1158. Strong, James. *Strong's Complete Dictionary of Bible Words.* Nashville: Thomas Nelson Publishers, 1996

plead. Plead is from the Greek word ἐντυγχάνω (entugchanó). It means to entreat (in favor or against); deal with; make intercession; to make petition. Source: Strong's Greek: #1793. Strong, James. *Strong's Complete Dictionary of Bible Words.* Nashville: Thomas Nelson Publishers, 1996

reconciliation. Reconciliation is simply the act of restoring a strained relationship, such as being reconciled to God the Father through Jesus Christ. Source: https://www.abibleaday.com/bible-dictionary/reconciliation/

redeem. Means to buy back or secure the freedom of someone in bondage. Source: https://www.dictionary.com/browse/redeemed.

regenerated. New birth; born again; born again spiritually. Source: Vine, W.E, Merrill F. Unger and William White, Jr. *Vine's Complete Expository Dictionary.* Nashville: Thomas Nelson, Inc., 1996

renew. To make new. Source: Vine, W.E, Merrill F. Unger and William White, Jr. *Vine's Complete Expository Dictionary.* Nashville: Thomas Nelson, Inc., 1996

seal. An identifying mark often placed on a letter, contract, or another document. Source: Raymond, Erik. *What Does It Mean to Be Sealed with the Holy Spirit?* Deerfield: The Gospel Coalition, INC, 2019. https://www.thegospelcoalition.org/blogs/erik-raymond/mean-sealed-holy-spirit/. (Accessed June 26, 2021).

sprinkled. The word sprinkled is from "zaraq zaw-rak" and means s to scatter or slightly drizzle in small measures.

unction. The act of anointing as a rite of consecration or healing; something used for anointing; a religious or spiritual fervor or the expression of such fervor (https://www.merriam-webster.com/dictionary/unction)

BOOKS AND ARTICLES RESEARCHED AND STUDIED

Adema, Ron. *Renewal of the Holy Spirit*. 2005. http://www. doctrinalstudies.com/pdf/D050619.pdf (Accessed November 28, 2021)

All About GOD Ministries. *All About Following Jesus. God's Forgiveness*. Belen: All About GOD Ministries, Inc. https://www.allaboutfollowingjesus.org/gods-forgiveness.htm. (Accessed September 4, 2021)

Answers In Genesis. https://answersingenesis.org/. (Accessed March 17, 2021)

Applying the Blood of Jesus. https://fromtheheartogod.files. wordpress.com/2014/04/blood_of_jesus.pdf. (Accessed October 15, 2021)

Babalola, Peter Adeshina. *Pleading the Blood of Jesus*. PowerTalk, 2018. http://www.powertalk.com.ng/2018/07/08/ pleading-the-blood-of-jesus/. (Accessed September 6, 2021)

Banso, T.O. *Ten Reasons a Child of God Should Rejoice*. Abuja, Nigeria: Cedar Ministry International, 2018 https:// cedarministry.org/ten-reasons-a-child-of-god-should-rejoice/ (Accessed April 18, 2021)

Bardsley, Rosemary. *The Great I Am. Jehovah-nissi: The Lord is My Banner*. God's Word For You, 2013. https://www.

godswordforyou.com/thoughts/the-great-i-am/711-the-lord-is-my-banner.html. (Accessed June 13, 2021)

Beeke, Joel. *My God, My God, Why Hast Thou Forsaken Me?.* Sanford: Table Talk, 2017. https://www.ligonier.org/blog/christ-forsaken/. (Accessed April 4, 2021)

Benek, Christopher, Reverend Doctor. *God Can Be Found In Difference Between Happiness and Joy.* Hilton Head Island: The Island Packet, 2014. https://www.islandpacket.com/living/religion/article33609807.html (Accessed April 18, 2021)

DeHaan, Peter. Bible Dictionary. https://www.abibleaday.com/bible-dictionary/. (Accessed March 14, 2021)

Bible Doctrines. Comstock Park: Bible Doctrines To Live By. https://www.bibledoctrines.org/. (Accessed March 17, 2021)

Bibles for America. *3 Problems Only the Blood of Jesus Can Solve.* Irvin: Bibles for America, 2020. https://blog.biblesforamerica.org/3-problems-that-can-only-be-solved-by-the-blood-of-jesus/. (Accessed August 29, 2021)

Bibles for America. *Knowing the Truth of God's Cleansing.* Irvin: Bibles for America, 2017. https://blog.biblesforamerica.org/knowing-gods-cleansing/. (Accessed January 22, 2022)

BibleRef. *What Does 1 John 3:9 Mean?* https://www.bibleref.com/1-John/3/1-John-3-9.html. (Accessed July 7, 2021)

Bible Study Tools. https://www.biblestudytools.com/. (Accessed March 14, 2021)

Bradley, Michael. *The Full Surrender.* Bible Knowledge, 2021. https://www.bible-knowledge.com/the-full-surrender/. (Accessed September 26, 2021)

Bradley, Michael. *God Will Guide Your Steps.* Bible Knowledge, 2021. https://www.bible-knowledge.com/god-s-guidance/. (Accessed October 31, 2021)

Bradley, Michael. *How to Plead the Blood of Jesus for Deliverance and Protection.* Bible Knowledge, 2021. https://www.bible-knowledge.com/blood-of-jesus-how-to-plead-for-protection-and-deliverance/. (Accessed September 25, 2021)

Brodie, Jessica. *What Does it Mean to Be Washed in the Blood?* Crosswalk, 2021. https://www.crosswalk.com/faith/spiritual-life/what-does-it-mean-to-be-washed-in-the-blood.html. (Accessed January 22, 2022)

Calvin, John. *What Does The 'Washing Of Regeneration' Refer To?* Bible Debates, 2018. https://bibledebates.wordpress.com/2018/01/25/what-does-the-washing-of-regeneration-refer-to/. (Accessed November 28, 2021)

Camarin, Juli. *The Mystery of His Will—Ephesians 1:9-10.* Juli Camarin JCBlog.net, 2015. https://www.jcblog.net/ephesians/1/9-10-the-mystery-of-his-will. (Accessed July 4, 2021)

Cole, Steven. *Lesson 3: He Chose Us (Ephesians 1:4).* Bible.org, 2013. https://bible.org/seriespage/lesson-3-he-chose-us-ephesians-14. (Accessed June 30, 2021)

Copeland, Kenneth. *The Power of the Blood of Jesus.* Kenneth Copeland Ministries. https://www.kcm.org/read/testimony/the-powerful-blood-jesus. (Accessed February, 21 2021)

Curt Landry. *How to Plead the Blood of Jesus.* Fairland: Curt Landry Ministries, 2021. https://www.curtlandry.com/how-to-plead-the-blood-of-jesus/#.YWQxdl7PzIU. (Accessed October 11, 2021)

Dake, Finis, Jennings. *Dake's Annotated Reference Bible* (Ninth Printing edition). Lawrenceville: Dake Publishing, Inc, 2006

Erin. *How To Surrender To God – Tearing Down Your Kingdom.* Raise Your Sword, 2021 https://raiseyoursword. com/how-to-surrender-to-god/. (Accessed September 12, 2021)

Fairchild, Mary. "The Blood of Jesus." Learn Religions. New York: Learn Religions, 2021,https://www.learnreligions. com/blood-of-jesus-700166. (Accessed on February 19, 2021)

Richison, Grant. *Galatians 6:17.* Verse By Verse Commentary, 2020. https://versebyversecommentary. com/2000/06/23/galatians-617/ (Accessed June 6, 2021)

Getty, Keith & Kristyn. "The Power of the Cross." Produced by John Schreiner. *Album In Christ Alone.* https://www.elyrics.net/read/k/keith-&-kristyn-getty-lyrics/the-power-of-the-cross-lyrics.html#:~:text=KEITH%20%26%20KRISTYN%20GETTY.%20The%20Power%20Of%20The,beaten%2C%20then.%20Nailed%20to%20a%20cross%20of%20wood. (Accessed March 21, 2021)

Goll, James. *7 Benefits of the Blood of Jesus.* Awakening Magazine, 2019. https://awakeningmag.com/7-benefits-of-the-blood-of-jesus/. (Accessed September 9, 2021)

Got Questions. *What Are Spiritual Blessings?* Got Questions Ministries. https://www.gotquestions.org/spiritual-blessings.html. (Accessed June 27, 2021)

Got Questions. *What Does It Mean The Lord Is My Banner?* Got Questions Ministries. https://www.gotquestions.org/ Lord-is-my-banner.html. (Accessed June 13, 2021)

Got Questions. *What Is Our Inheritance in Christ?* Got Questions Ministries. https://www.gotquestions.org/inheritance-in-Christ.html. (Accessed August 8, 2021)

Got Questions. *In What Ways Are Believers Partakers Of The Divine Nature?* Got Questions Ministries. https://www.gotquestions.org/partakers-divine-nature.html. (Accessed December 4, 2021)

Got Questions. *Is Pleading the Blood of Jesus Biblical?* Got Questions Ministries. https://www.gotquestions.org/pleading-the-blood.html. (Accessed August 25, 2021)

Got Questions. *What Does It Mean That There Is No Condemnation In Christ (Romans 8:1)?* Got Questions Ministries. https://www.gotquestions.org/no-condemnation.html. (Accessed July 7, 2021)

Got Questions. *What Does It Mean To Be "Whiter Than Snow" (Psalm 51:7)?* Got Questions Ministries. https://www.gotquestions.org/whiter-than-snow.html. (Accessed January 22, 2022)

Got Questions. *What Is Hyssop?* Got Questions Ministries. https://www.gotquestions.org/hyssop-Bible.html. (Accessed January 22, 2022)

Got Questions. *What Is Regeneration According To The Bible?* Got Questions Ministries. https://www.gotquestions.org/regeneration-Bible.html. (Accessed November 28, 2021)

Got Questions. *Why is Giving Thanks to God Important?* Got Questions Ministries. https://www.gotquestions.org/giving-thanks-to-God.html. (Accessed January 8, 2023)

Hagin, Kenneth W. *I Plead the Blood!* Broken Arrow: Kenneth Hagin Ministries, 2020. https://events.rhema.org/i-plead-the-blood/. (Accessed September 6, 2021)

Haworth, Elizabeth. *The Divine Life.* Knowing Jesus, 2021. https://devotion.knowing-jesus.com/the-divine-life. (Accessed December 9, 2021)

Hayford, Jack. *Pleading the Blood.* Van Nuys: Jack Hayford Ministries. https://www.jackhayford.org/teaching/articles/pleading-the-blood/. (Accessed September 5, 2021)

Hayford, Jack. *Spirit Filled Life Bible for Students.* New King James Version. Nashville: Thomas Nelson Publishers, 1982

Henderson, Robert. *Operating In the Courts of Heaven.* Shippensburg: Destiny Image Publishers, Inc., 2021

Holm, Thomas. *Is It Biblical to Plead the Blood of Jesus?* https://thejosephplan.org/is-it-biblical-to-plead-the-blood-of-jesus/. (Accessed September 12, 2021)

Holm, Thomas. *How to Plead and Pray The Blood of Jesus Prayer for Protection.* The Joseph Plan, 2017. https://thejosephplan.org/how-to-plead-and-pray-the-blood-of-jesus-prayer-spiritual-warfare/. (Accessed September 12, 2021)

Jones, Lewis E. *There Is Power In the Blood.* Guthrie: Faith Publishing House, Evening Light Songs, 1949, edited 1987. https://library.timelesstruths.org/music/There_Is_Power_in_the_Blood/.

Kaywood, David. *Bible Signs & Symbols "Blood".* Jacksonville Beach: Jesus Way 4 You, 2015. https://jesusway4you.com/2015/09/29/bible-signs-symbols-blood/. (Accessed on June 4, 2021)

Kraft, Charles H. *I Give You Authority.* Grand Rapids: Chosen Books, A Division of Baker Book House Company, 2000

Kirk, Bill. *The Place Called "Calvary" (What Actually Happened When Jesus Died?).* http://enjoythejourneysermons.com/wp-content/uploads/2015/01/the-place-called-calvary.pdf. (Accessed March 21, 2021)

Knowing Jesus. *The Cleansing Word.* https://dailyverse.know-ing-jesus.com/john-15-3. (Accessed November 21, 2021)

Knowing Jesus. *What Does Acts 26:18 Mean?* https://daily-verse.knowing-jesus.com/acts-26-18. (Accessed August 22, 2021)

Knowing Jesus. *What Does Revelation 1:5 Mean?* https://dailyverse.knowing-jesus.com/revelation-1-5. (Accessed January 22, 2022)

LaHaye, Tim. *Prophecy Study Bible.* New King James Version, Chattanooga: AMG Publishers, 2000

LeClaire, Jennifer. *Decrees That Make the Devil Flee.* Fort Lauderdale: Awakening Media, 2020

Lee, Witness. *The Renewing of the Holy Spirit. To Reconstitute Our Being on the Positive Side.* Anaheim: Living Stream Ministry. https://www.ministrysamples.org/excerpts/THE-RENEWING-OF-THE-HOLY-SPIRIT-TO-RECONSTITUTE-OUR-BEING-ON-THE-POSITIVE-SIDE.HTML. (Accessed December 3, 2021)

Marie, Elizabeth. *Spiritual Warfare Tactic — Appropriate the Blood of Jesus.* His Kingdom Prophecy, 2019. https://www.hiskingdomprophecy.com/spiritual-warfare-tactic-appro-priate-the-blood-of-jesus/. (Accessed September 19, 2021)

Mathis, David. *The Precious Power of the Blood. Five Benefits Christ Purchased for You.* Desiring God, 2019. https://www.desiringgod.org/articles/the-precious-power-of-the-blood. (Accessed February 18, 2021)

Melanie. *11 Ways to Surrender to God + FREE 30-Day Surrender Challenge Printable.* Wildly Anchored. https://www.wildlyanchored.com/ways-to-surrender-to-god/. (Accessed September 13, 2021)

Merkle, Benjamin L. *What Does It Mean That God Chose Us before the Foundation of the World? (Ephesians 1).*

Crossway, 2020. https://www.crossway.org/articles/what-does-it-mean-that-god-chose-us-before-the-foundation-of-the-world-ephesians-1/. (Accessed July 4, 2021)

Oliver, Evelyn. *Christian Questions. "Why Do Christians Plead The Blood Of Jesus? Explained."* Just Disciples. https://justdisciple.com/chrisitans-plead-blood-jesus/#:~:text=Why%20do%20Christians%20plead%20the%20blood%20of%20Jesus%3F,more%20likely%20for%20God%20to%20fulfill%20that%20prayer. (Accessed August 25, 2021)

Piper, Barnabas. *The Meaning of Jehovah Nissi and the Significance of God's Name for Today.* Bible Study Tools, 2021. https://www.biblestudytools.com/bible-study/topical-studies/jehovah-nissi-the-lord-is-my-banner.html. (Accessed June 13, 2021)

Poblete, Chris. *Salvation: Past, Present, Future.* Blue Letter Bible Blog, 2012. https://blogs.blueletterbible.org/blb/2012/11/13/salvation-past-present-future/. (Accessed August 1, 2021)

Prince, Derek. *The Blood of the Lamb.* Derek Prince Ministries. https://www.derekprince.com/teaching/11-3. (Accessed November 28, 2021)

Prince, Joseph. *You Are Accepted in the Beloved.* Ft. Mill: Joseph Prince Ministries. https://www.josephprince.com/meditate-devo/you-are-accepted-in-the-beloved. (Accessed July 4, 2021)

Raymond, Erik. *What Does It Mean to Be Sealed with the Holy Spirit?* Deerfield: The Gospel Coalition, INC, 2019. https://www.thegospelcoalition.org/blogs/erik-raymond/mean-sealed-holy-spirit/. (Accessed June 26, 2021)

Regoli, Natalie. *Galatians 2:20 Meaning of Crucified with Christ.* Washington, DC: Connect Us Fund, 2020.

https://connectusfund.org/galatians-2-20-meaning-of-crucified-with-christ. (Accessed June 26, 2021)

Regoli, Natalie. *Washing of Water by the Word Meaning and Meditation*. Washington, DC: Connect Us Fund, 2021. https://connectusfund.org/washing-of-water-by-the-word-meaning. (Accessed November 25, 2021)

Rohrbaugh, Jamie. *How To Get Your Prayers Answered 100% of the Time.* From His Presence. https://www.fromhispresence.com/how-to-get-your-prayers-answered-100-of-the-time/. (Accessed November 7, 2021)

Rohrbaugh, Jamie. *How To Plead the Blood of Jesus in Prayer.* https://www.ibelieve.com/faith/how-to-plead-the-blood-of-jesus-in-prayer.html. (Accessed October 11, 2021)

Shepherd's Notes. *When You Need a Guide Through the Scriptures*. Nashville: Broadman & Holman Publishers, 1998

Spurgeon, Charles, H. *The Blood of Abel and the Blood of Jesus.* Answers In Genesis, 2011. https://answersingenesis.org/education/spurgeon-sermons/708-the-blood-of-abel-and-the-blood-of-jesus. (Accessed February 14, 2021)

Spurgeon, Charles, H. *The Blood of Sprinkling*. Blue Letter Bible. https://www.blueletterbible.org/Comm/spurgeon_charles/sermons/1888.cfm. (Accessed January 17, 2022)

Stanley, Charles F. *God's Purpose for Your Life*. Nashville: Thomas Nelson Publishers, 2020

Stanley, Charles F. "No Condemnation." *In Touch,* October 2021

Stanley, Charles F. "The Cost of Our Salvation." *In Touch,* February 2022

Stanley, Charles F. "The Cross: Grace Displayed." *In Touch,* May 2019

Stanley, Charles F. "The Good News About Death." *In Touch,* February 2021

Stanley, Charles F. *The Message of the Blood of Jesus Christ.* In Touch Ministries. https://youtu.be/EVxYNzjEH58. (Accessed February 19, 2021)

Stanley, Charles F. "A Yielded Life." *In Touch,* October 2021

Strong, James. *Strong's Complete Dictionary of Bible Words.* Nashville: Thomas Nelson Publishers, 1996

Tenney Tommy and T.F. Tenney. *Secret Sources of Power.* Shippensburg: Destiny Image Publishers, Inc, 2000

Vine, W.E, Merrill F. Unger and William White, Jr. *Vine's Complete Expository Dictionary.* Nashville: Thomas Nelson, Inc., 1996

Wellman, Jack. *What Is Sanctification?* What Christians Want To Know. https://www.whatchristianswanttoknow.com/what-is-sanctification-a-bible-study/#ixzz6pO8hwr4O (Accessed March 17, 2021)

What Is The Sprinkling of 1 Peter 1:2? McMinnville: The Gospel of Christ. https://www.thegospelofchrist.com/knowledge-base/tgoc-kb—6328t. (Accessed January 17, 2022)

Wilson, Walter. *A Dictionary of Bible Types.* Peabody: Hendrickson Publishers, Inc, 1999

Winkler, Kyle. *Blood is Mentioned Throughout the Bible. But Why? The Answer is Incredible!* God TV, 2019. https://godtv.com/blood-is-mentioned-throughout-the-bible-but-why-the-answer-is-incredible/. (Accessed on April 25,2021)

ABOUT THE AUTHOR

Anthony (Tony) Powell gave his life to Jesus Christ in July 1999. In His Image Christian Ministries (IHICM) ordained and commissioned him as an elder to teach and preach the Word and administer the sacraments, ordinances, and other church functions. He serves at IHICM in various capacities, such as Elder, Teacher, and Director of Evangelism and Scholarship Ministries. He is also a faculty member and Prophetic Presbyter of Bishop R. S. Walker Ministries School of the Prophets. Additionally, he is the author of *I Am Fearfully and Wonderfully Made* which provides a biblically based foundation to understand that the eternal Father fearfully and wonderfully made us in His image and likeness and gave us an identity so we can fulfill three realities: to God be the glory, I can do what the Word says I can do and by the grace of God, I am what I am.

CPSIA information can be obtained
at www.ICGtesting.com
Printed in the USA
LVHW080725310323
743076LV00010B/94